Moodle Gradebook

Set up and customize the gradebook to track student progress through Moodle

Rebecca Barrington

[PACKT] open source *
PUBLISHING   community experience distilled

BIRMINGHAM - MUMBAI

Moodle Gradebook

First published: April 2012

Production Reference: 1300312

Published by Packt Publishing Ltd.
Livery Place
35 Livery Street
Birmingham B3 2PB, UK..

ISBN 978-1-84951-814-7

www.packtpub.com

Cover Image by Asher Wishkerman (a.wishkerman@mpic.de)

Credits

Author

Rebecca Barrington

Reviewers

Carol Hampton

Jim Judges

Acquisition Editor

Sarah Cullington

Lead Technical Editor

Susmita Panda

Technical Editor

Naheed Shaikh

Project Coordinator

Vishal Bodwani

Proofreader

Martin Diver

Indexer

Tejal Daruwale

Production Coordinator

Melwyn D'sa

Cover Work

Melwyn D'sa

About the Author

Rebecca Barrington has been using Moodle for over seven years while working at South Devon College. She provides a range of support, training, and information guides for teaching staff. She uses Moodle in her own teaching, including a qualification about virtual learning environments. Rebecca has a keen interest in using technologies to support learning and is continually developing new ways of using Moodle and applying these to online courses for use with students.

South Devon College has a reputation for its use of technology, and Rebecca also travelled around the country to deliver training and advice on using Moodle to other organizations as well as at regional and national events. She is also a regular contributor to online VLE forums to share ideas and advice.

Follow Rebecca on Twitter: @bbarrington

I would like to thank my family and friends, in particular Maria, Rob, Marilyn, and Dave, for checking that the information I had written made sense before I shared it with anyone else. I would also like to thank Bayley, Emilie, and Ava for allowing me to use their names (and their parents who gave their consent). I should also say hello to Madeline who would also have been in the book but was only born while I was writing the fourth chapter!

I would like to thank South Devon College for allowing me to write this book and, in particular, Paul Vaughan, who ensured that I had the latest versions of Moodle to play with!

I would also like to thank all at PacktPub, especially the reviewers, for their support while writing my first book.

About the Reviewers

Carol Hampton works at her local college as an Educational Technologist. She encourages and supports staff to use different technologies within their teaching. Moodle is one of the larger areas she helps staff with, and the has been involved with the implementation and upkeep of their Moodle since 2005. She has worked, in collaboration, on a number of projects with other colleges in her region, as well as internationally.

Jim Judges is a freelance eLearning consultant. He has previously worked as a Lecturer in Further and Higher Education, a Teaching and Learning Development Manager, JISC eLearning Adviser, and Senior Lecturer and Partnership Manager at Birmingham City University. He has been using Moodle to support teaching and learning since 2006, and continues to develop and deliver a range of face-to-face training and online courses using Moodle.

Since 2010, he has worked as an eLearning Associate for the University of London Computer Centre (ULCC), and as a consultant and trainer for a range of clients, including UK-based Moodle partners.

He lives in the Midlands, UK, with his wife Jo and two teenage daughters.

www.PacktPub.com

Support files, eBooks, discount offers and more

You might want to visit www.PacktPub.com for support files and downloads related to your book.

Did you know that Packt offers eBook versions of every book published, with PDF and ePub files available? You can upgrade to the eBook version at www.PacktPub.com and as a print book customer, you are entitled to a discount on the eBook copy. Get in touch with us at service@packtpub.com for more details.

At www.PacktPub.com, you can also read a collection of free technical articles, sign up for a range of free newsletters and receive exclusive discounts and offers on Packt books and eBooks.

http://PacktLib.PacktPub.com

Do you need instant solutions to your IT questions? PacktLib is Packt's online digital book library. Here, you can access, read and search across Packt's entire library of books.

Why Subscribe?

- Fully searchable across every book published by Packt
- Copy and paste, print and bookmark content
- On demand and accessible via web browser

Free Access for Packt account holders

If you have an account with Packt at www.PacktPub.com, you can use this to access PacktLib today and view nine entirely free books. Simply use your login credentials for immediate access.

Table of Contents

Preface

Moodle is used in many areas of education to provide a range of resources and activities to support learning. However, it can also be used to manage learning and record progress.

This book will explain the uses of the Moodle grades area, also known as the Gradebook, to record grades for work completed and to calculate final grades. You will also learn the different options for grading work, customizing how the grades appear, and how to view progress through a range of reports. This book is based on Moodle 2.2 and will highlight some of the new features within Moodle 2 that complement the gradebook. However, many of the general gradebook instructions will also be useful for Moodle 1.9 users as the core gradebook is the same within both versions.

The book will provide step-by-step instructions, with screenshots, to take you through setting up the gradebook, adding tasks with grades, and reporting progress.

What this book covers

This book is an introduction to the gradebook and how it can be used to manage assessment. It does not explain every option possible within the **Grades** area and activities, as there are too many! However, it will cover the most commonly used elements that can be used and adapted to meet most course needs.

Chapter 1, Introduction to the Gradebook: In this chapter, you will be given an overview of the different elements of the gradebook and how they apply to an online course. This will set the scene for the practical instructions throughout the book.

Chapter 2, Customizing the Grades: In this chapter, you can follow the step-by-step instructions on how to create your own custom scale (using statements rather than numbers) and use letter grades (letters or words linked to a percentage). Outcomes will also be explained to enable more detailed recording within assessments.

Chapter 3, Adding Graded Activities: In this chapter, you will learn how to add grading options to assignments and also the use of advanced grading methods to enable grading using multiple criteria.

Chapter 4, Assigning Grades: This chapter will demonstrate the various ways in which assessments can be marked with written feedback and grades.

Chapter 5, Using Calculations: In this chapter, we will take a look at using the gradebook to calculate final grades for online courses. We will review the different options available and how each one can be used.

Chapter 6, Organizing Using Categories: In this chapter, we will add categories into the gradebook and move assignments into them. We will also look at ways of using categories to further customize how we use the gradebook.

Chapter 7, Reporting with the Gradebook: This chapter will show you the different reports available to view all grades or individual user information, plus how to export the gradebook data.

Chapter 8, Additional Features for Progress Tracking: Finally, in this chapter, we will look at other features within Moodle 2 that complement the gradebook. We will use the activity and course completion features to provide a pictorial view of the student's achievement.

How to use this book

Users that are new to Moodle assessments and the gradebook can read the book from beginning to end and follow the instructions to get some practical experience. Users that are already familiar with the basics of the gradebook can use each chapter individually to customize the gradebook according to their needs.

If you would like to work through the instructions in this book, you will need editing access to a course in Moodle 2.2.

 You can also use the instructions if you are using an earlier version of Moodle, but the advanced grading/rubrics section of *Chapter 3, Adding Graded Activities*, should be ignored. The gradebook in Moodle 1.9 is also very similar to Moodle 2.x, so most of the instructions can still be followed, if you are using that version.

What you need for this book

This book assumes that you already know the following:

- How to access and navigate Moodle using the breadcrumb menu
- How to add resources and activities in Moodle

Some of the features and activities explained will need to be turned on in the administration settings. Where this is required, it will be explained how to do it in an information box.

Who this book is for

Moodle Gradebook is for anyone who uses Moodle as a course instructor. You will need to know the basic functions of using and navigating Moodle, but no prior knowledge of the grades functions will be required.

Conventions

In this book, you will find a number of styles of text that distinguish between different kinds of information. Here are some examples of these styles, and an explanation of their meaning.

New terms and **important words** are shown in bold. Words that you see on the screen, in menus or dialog boxes for example, appear in the text like this: "view the **Settings** block on the course".

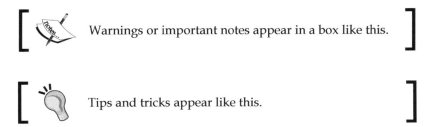

Warnings or important notes appear in a box like this.

Tips and tricks appear like this.

Reader feedback

Feedback from our readers is always welcome. Let us know what you think about this book—what you liked or may have disliked. Reader feedback is important for us to develop titles that you really get the most out of.

To send us general feedback, simply send an e-mail to feedback@packtpub.com, and mention the book title through the subject of your message.

If there is a topic that you have expertise in and you are interested in either writing or contributing to a book, see our author guide on www.packtpub.com/authors.

Customer support

Now that you are the proud owner of a Packt book, we have a number of things to help you to get the most from your purchase.

Errata

Although we have taken every care to ensure the accuracy of our content, mistakes do happen. If you find a mistake in one of our books—maybe a mistake in the text or the code—we would be grateful if you would report this to us. By doing so, you can save other readers from frustration and help us improve subsequent versions of this book. If you find any errata, please report them by visiting http://www.packtpub.com/support, selecting your book, clicking on the **errata submission form** link, and entering the details of your errata. Once your errata are verified, your submission will be accepted and the errata will be uploaded to our website, or added to any list of existing errata, under the Errata section of that title.

Piracy

Piracy of copyright material on the Internet is an ongoing problem across all media. At Packt, we take the protection of our copyright and licenses very seriously. If you come across any illegal copies of our works, in any form, on the Internet, please provide us with the location address or website name immediately so that we can pursue a remedy.

Please contact us at copyright@packtpub.com with a link to the suspected pirated material.

We appreciate your help in protecting our authors, and our ability to bring you valuable content.

Questions

You can contact us at questions@packtpub.com if you are having a problem with any aspect of the book, and we will do our best to address it.

Introduction to the Gradebook 1

If you are using Moodle, you are likely to be delivering some form of course content or providing resources to others. This could be for supporting learning, training, or other educational activity. Many online courses, qualifications, or educational resources have a final goal which is likely to include required elements to be completed. The gradebook can be a valuable tool to help the teacher to manage the online course and track the progress of the student through the required elements.

This chapter will introduce you to the gradebook and the key features it offers. It will outline the benefits of using the gradebook, the activities that can be graded and used within the gradebook, and the types of grades that can be used. You will be given an overview of how it can be used to manage learning before moving through the rest of the chapters to learn how to set up the different elements.

Getting to the gradebook

All courses in Moodle have a grades area, also known as the **gradebook**. A number of activities within Moodle can be graded and these grades will automatically be captured and shown in the gradebook.

To get to the gradebook, view the **Settings** block on the course and then click on **Grades**.

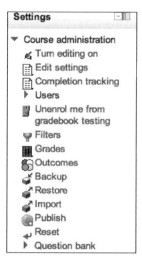

The following screenshot shows an example of the teachers' view of a simple gradebook with a number of different graded activities within it. Let's take a quick tour of what we can see!

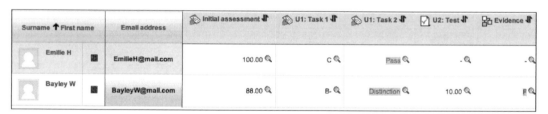

- The top row of the screenshot shows the column headings which are each of the assessed activities within the Moodle course. These automatically appear in the grades area. In this case, the assessed activities are:
    - **Initial assessment**
    - **U1: Task 1**
    - **U1: Task 2**
    - **U2: Test**
    - **Evidence**

- On the left of the screenshot, you can see the students' names. Essentially, the name is the start of a row of information about the student. If we start with **Emilie H**, we can see that she received a score of **100.00** for her **Initial assessment**.
- Looking at **Bayley W,** we can see that his work for **U1: Task 2** received a **Distinction** grade.

Using the gradebook, we can see all the assessments and grades linked to each student from one screen.

Users with teacher, non-editing teacher, or manager roles will be able to see the grades for all students on the course. Students will only be able to see their own grades and feedback.

The advantage of storing the grades within Moodle is that information can be easily shared between all teachers on the online course. Traditionally, if a course manager wanted to know how students were progressing they would need to contact the course teacher(s) to gather this information. Now, they can log in to Moodle and view the live data (as long as they have teacher or manager rights to the course).

There are also benefits to students as they will see all their progress in one place and can start to manage their own learning by reviewing their progress to date as shown in the following example of student view:

Grade Item	Grade	Range	Percentage	Feedback
Using the Gradebook to Manage Assessment				
Initial assessment	88.00	0–100	88.00 %	Well done.
U1: Task 1	B-	0–100	82.00 %	82% for this assignment. Well done. You could further improve your grade by discussing the issues with the theory.
U1: Task 2	Distinction	"Refer"–Distinction	100.00 %	
U2: Test	10.00	0–10	100.00 %	
Evidence	F	0–10	50.00 %	

This is Bayley W's grade report. Bayley can see each assessment on the left-hand side with his grade next to it. By default, the student grades report also shows the range of grades possible for the assessment (for example, the highest and lowest scores possible), but this can be switched off by the teacher in the **Grades** course settings. It also shows the equivalent percentage as well as the written feedback given by the teacher. The options for customizing reports will be explained further in *Chapter 7, Reporting with the Gradebook*.

Activities that work with the gradebook

There are a number of Moodle activities that can be graded and, therefore, work with the gradebook. The main ones are the following:

- Quiz
- Assignments: Four different core assignment types can be used to meet a range of needs within courses:
  - Advanced uploading of files
  - Online text
  - Upload a single file
  - Offline activity (The offline assignment is particularly useful for practical qualifications or presentations where the assessment is not submitted and is assessed offline by the teacher. The offline activity allows the detail of the assessment to be provided to students in Moodle, and the grade and feedback to be stored in the gradebook, even though no work has been electronically submitted.)

Encouraging the use of the gradebook

The offline activity is often a good way to start using the gradebook to record progress, as the assessment can take place in the normal way, but the grades can be recorded centrally to benefit teachers and students. Once confident with using the gradebook, teachers can then review assessment processes to use other assignment types.

- Forum
- Lesson
- SCORM package
- Workshop
- Glossary

It is also possible to manually set up a "graded item" within the gradebook that is not linked with an activity, but allows a grade to be recorded.

This book will not explain how to add these activities. However, *Chapter 3, Adding Graded Activities*, will provide an overview of how to choose customized options within an assignment. The core elements of adding activities within Moodle are very similar, so these instructions can be used to add the same options within the other activity types.

Key features of the gradebook

The gradebook primarily shows the grade or score for each graded activity within the online course. This grade could be shown in a number of ways:

- **Numeric grade**: A numerical grade between 1 and 100. This is already set up and ready to use within all Moodle courses.
- **Scale**: A customized grading profile that can be letters, words, statements, or numbers (such as **Pass**, **Merit**, and **Distinction**).
- **Letter grade**: A grading profile that can be linked to percentages (such as 100 percent = A).

Within some activities (such as the assignments), written feedback can be provided in addition to the grade and can be viewed in the user reports and by students.

Organizing grades

With lots of activities that use grades within a course, the gradebook can be a lot of data on one page. **Categories** can be created to group activities and the gradebook view can be customized according to the user to see all or some categories on the screen.

Think about a course that has 15 units and each unit has three assessments within it. The gradebook will have 45 columns of grades – which is a lot of data! We can organize this information into categories to make it easier to use. We will be doing this in Chapter 6, *Organizing Using Categories*.

Summary

This chapter has given you a brief overview of the gradebook, what it will show, how it can be used, and which activities feed into the grades area. It has only provided an introduction to the key features, but you will now work through each chapter to learn how to set them up.

As each element is explained in the following chapters, activities will be provided to enable us to apply the ideas as well as providing a range of example uses. The default settings will be used initially for examples, but where further customization is required, this will be explained within the chapters. These settings will mainly be changed at course level by a course teacher, but where these settings need to be turned on by an administrator this will also be highlighted.

In the next chapter, you will find out more about the different grading options and scales and have a go at customizing scales and letter grades.

2
Customizing the Grades

When creating a graded activity, you will choose how the activity will be scored, and this score will automatically be added into the course grades area.

The default grading options in a Moodle site are number grades (0-100) and a preset scale called "separate and connected ways of knowing". However, different courses will use different grading conventions and the ability to customize grades to meet specific course needs is sometimes necessary. Scales and letter grades can be customized by course and sitewide scales can be set by your Moodle administrator.

In this chapter, the different grading options will be outlined and you will be given some example uses of each grade type. You will create your own custom scales using words or statements, customize the letter grades, and set up outcomes. The considerations for calculating final grades and adding grades together will also be outlined in relation to each grade type.

Numeric grades

100 is the default grade for all assessments in Moodle. When setting up a graded activity, you will choose the highest grade possible for that assignment (such as 50) and, when marking the work, you will assign the grade achieved. No other changes need to be made in order to use numerical grades.

Numeric grades are the simplest type of grading for calculating course scores. Numbers are always easier to add than words!

Letter grades

Some assessments or homework activities, such as GCSE subjects, may need to be graded with a letter such A or D. In Moodle, letter grades are essentially number grades that are shown as letters in the gradebook. The advantage of using letter grades is that they act like numbers, so can be used for course total calculations.

The default grade letters within Moodle courses are shown as follows:

Edit grade letters		
Highest	**Lowest**	**Letter**
100.00 %	93.00 %	A
92.99 %	90.00 %	A-
89.99 %	87.00 %	B+
86.99 %	83.00 %	B
82.99 %	80.00 %	B-
79.99 %	77.00 %	C+
76.99 %	73.00 %	C
72.99 %	70.00 %	C-
69.99 %	67.00 %	D+
66.99 %	60.00 %	D
59.99 %	0.00 %	F
Edit grade letters		

When the teacher grades the work, they give a numerical grade which is then converted by Moodle into a percentage and shown as the relevant grade letter in the gradebook.

For example: If the course uses the default letter grades and an assignment is given a grade of 85 percent, the letter grade shown in the gradebook would be B because the grade is between **83.00%** and **86.99%**, as shown in the previous screenshot.

The letter grades can be customized to link to any percentage in order to meet the course needs. The letters can also be changed into words.

Customizing letter grades

Let's set up an example together and see an alternative use of the letter grades.

Creating a letter grade that uses words

In this example, we are going to set up letter grades to enable teachers to grade the work out of 36, which will be the grade required in order to gain a distinction for each assessment. However, if the student does not meet all the criteria, they can gain a lower grade (either a pass or a merit). If they don't meet enough criteria, the work would be graded as not yet complete. The teacher will score the assignment with the numbers, but the students will see the word as their grade. When we come to set up the final course total, Moodle will make use of the numbers to calculate the final grade based on the aggregation (the calculation) we choose.

In order to ensure that the letter grades show **Pass, Merit,** or **Distinction,** we need to customize the letter grades to show these words and identify the equivalent percentage for the differing pass levels. The following table shows the final grade linked to the different pass grades and the calculated percentage:

Grade	Minimum grade	Percentage
Distinction	36	100% (36/36*100)
Merit	27	75% (27/36*100)
Pass	18	50% (18/36*100)
Not yet complete	Below 18	49.9% or lower

 The percentage is calculated through the following formula: minimum grade divided by maximum grade (in this case 36) and multiplied by 100.

The percentages used in letter grades are set to two decimal places and require a maximum and minimum percentage per letter grade. The full range needs to extend from 0.00 percent to 100.00 percent.

So, lets set this up in a course!

1. Within the course click on the **Settings** block.

2. Click on **Grades**.

3. Once in the grades area, you will either see a drop-down list, tabs, or both (the view you will see will depend on the settings made by your site administrator. The default setting is the drop-down menu only, but this can be changed by changing the **Navigation method** in **Site administration | Grades | General** settings). If using the **Grader report** drop-down list, find the heading **Letters** and click on **View**. If using the tabs, click on **Letters**.

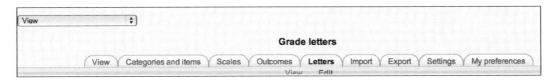

4. Click on **Edit grade letters**.

5. Click on **Override site defaults** so that a tick appears in the box.

We need to set the grade letter and grade boundary for each item that we would like to use in the course. Use the table showing the percentages for Pass, Merit, and Distinction (mentioned previously) to set up the grade letters as shown in the following screenshot. The grade boundary is the minimum score required to get that grade. Start from the top (**100%**) and work down the list. Once you have added 0%, all the other letter grades need to be set as unused. You do not need to worry about removing any grade letters shown in the grade letter field. They will simply be ignored once the grade letter boundary drop-down list has been set to unused.

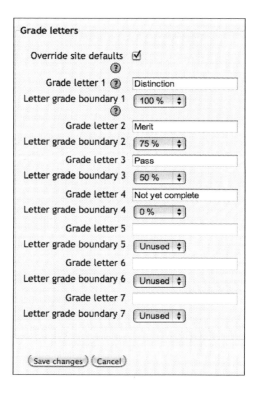

6. Click on **Save changes** and you will see a table similar to the one shown in the following screenshot. If you need to change these grades at any time, you can click on **Edit grade letters** or, if you are in the main course screen, you can go to **Settings | Grades**, click on the **Grader report** drop-down menu, find **Letters,** and click on **Edit.**

These letter grades are now set up to use on the course.

Edit grade letters		
Highest	**Lowest**	**Letter**
100.00 %	100.00 %	Distinction
99.99 %	75.00 %	Merit
74.99 %	50.00 %	Pass
49.99 %	0.00 %	Not yet complete

Note that by adding the grade boundaries (in this case the minimum score required to gain each grade), Moodle will calculate the maximum percentage to ensure the grade profile ranges from **0.00%** to **100.00%**.

When we come to set up a graded activity that shows the letters, we will also need to make some changes within the gradebook.

Only one set of letter grades can be used per course. Therefore, whenever letter grades are used, they will always use the letters set up for that course. So in the course that we are using in this example, now that we have set up the pass, merit, and distinction letter grades, the original default A – D plus F grading (shown in the first screenshot in this chapter) will no longer be available within this course. You can, however, have multiple scales within your course.

Scales

Scales are a list of words or characters that can be used to grade work. Each scale needs at least two choices, but you can have as many options in the scale as you want. You can also use lots of different scales within one course. Examples of scales could include:

- Refer, pass
- Unsatisfactory, satisfactory, good, outstanding
- Reviewed, feedback given
- A, B, C, D, E, F
- Fail, pass, merit, distinction

The scale is created prior to the graded activity being added to the course and, when an activity is added to the course, the required scale can be selected. When marking work, the teacher is given the scale options in a drop-down list, so that they can select the grade to be awarded.

Scales are useful when work is assessed using words or phrases or when a course needs to use a range of grades to provide feedback to learners (as letter grades will only let you have one option per course).

Scales can still be used for calculating final grades, but the scores are based on the number of items in the scale rather than a specific score for each element of the scale. When used to calculate course totals, the grading used for calculations is based on the number of items in a scale. Think about a simple scale containing two options: *Complete* and *Not complete*. In this example, the scale would be based on a highest score of 2 (1 point for not complete and 2 points for complete), or it could be based on a score of 0 for not complete and 1 point for complete. How the score is used depends on the category aggregation we choose (which we will look at in more detail in *Chapter 5, Using Calculations*).

Calculating scores using scales can be confusing and therefore scales are not always the best option when complex scoring is required. However, for courses that use simple calculations, or where there is a point at which a learner will *pass*, scales can be a useful way to present course grades to students that will make sense to them.

Customizing grade scales

In the example used earlier, we used pass, merit, and distinction as grade letters, but this could also easily be added as a word scale. We will set this one up as a scale to see how the scoring would be different.

1. Within the course, click on the **Settings** block.
2. Click on **Grades**.
3. Once in the grades area, you will either see a drop-down list or tabs (or both). If using the drop-down list, find the heading **Scales** and click on **View**. If using the tabs, click **Scales**.
4. At the bottom of this screen, click on **Add a new scale**.
5. In the **Name** box, give the scale a title. In this case, give it the name **PMD** to identify it as pass, merit, and distinction. This name is used when we choose to use the scale; hence, it needs to be easily identified and differentiated from any other scales available.

 If you would like a scale that is available sitewide, an administrator also has the option of setting this as a **Standard scale** by putting a tick into the box. Teachers will not be able to choose this option.

6. In the **Scale** box, we will write each word that we would like to appear in the grading list with each one separated by a comma. It needs to start with a negative scale item and end with a positive scale item (that is, the first scale item should be the lowest grade, which increases gradually until it equals the scale item with the highest grade). In this example, complete the **Scale** box as shown in the following screenshot:

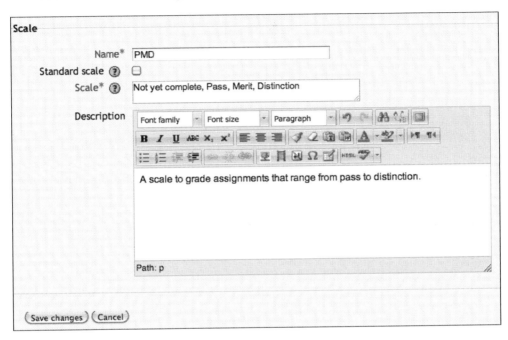

7. In the **Description** box, provide a brief explanation of the scale and/or its use. This is particularly important for standard (sitewide) scales, as teachers may choose to use it even though they haven't created it themselves.

8. Click on **Save changes** to save this scale. This scale is now available to use.

We will look at how this will be scored when we look at category aggregation in *Chapter 5, Using Calculations*. However, it will be one of the following two grading profiles:

Not yet complete	Pass	Merit	Distinction
0	1	2	3
1	2	3	4

You can see how this will be calculated differently from the letter grade percentages used earlier.

Have another go!

Let's also set up a simple scale that we can use later so that we can practice adding these custom scales.

Create a scale called **Completion** with three options: **Not yet complete**, **Partially complete**, and **Complete**. Remember to add them in a negative to positive order.

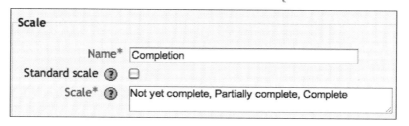

Using outcomes

Outcomes are extra elements that can be added to a graded activity to be able to grade whether specific elements have been completed. Each outcome can be graded with a scale, but the teacher must also put in an overall grade for the graded activity. Outcomes can be especially useful for courses that require students to demonstrate competency against specific performance criteria. When we add a graded activity, we will choose which outcomes, if any, it links with (you do not have to use all outcomes on all assessments).

We will set up some outcomes to enable us to assess whether specific criteria is completed and evidence is provided. We will make use of the **Completion** scale that we have just set up.

In order for outcomes to be set up in a course, they need to be enabled sitewide by an administrator. The setting can be turned on by adding a tick next to **Enable outcomes**, under **Site administration | Advanced features**. Click on **Save changes** at the bottom of the screen. Once this has been done, an **Outcomes** option will appear in the course settings block.

We will create three outcomes that we can use to assess elements of the assignment. These will be:

- Criteria 1 met
- Criteria 2 met
- Evidence provided

Let's add the outcomes!

1. Within the course, click on the **Settings** block.
2. Click on **Grades**.
3. Once in the grades area, you will either see a drop-down list or tabs as before. If using the drop-down list, find the heading **Outcomes** and click on **Edit outcomes**. If using the tabs, click **Outcomes** and click on **Edit outcomes** at the bottom of the screen.
4. Click on **Add a new outcome**.
5. We will use the same name for the **Full name** and **Short name** boxes to prevent confusion later (the **Short name** is only used in the outcomes report, but it is best to keep the **Full name** short too as this will show in the gradebook). We will keep both the names short!
6. In the **Full name** and **Short name** box, type in *evidence provided*. We need to add the outcomes in reverse order to ensure they appear in the correct order in the gradebook.

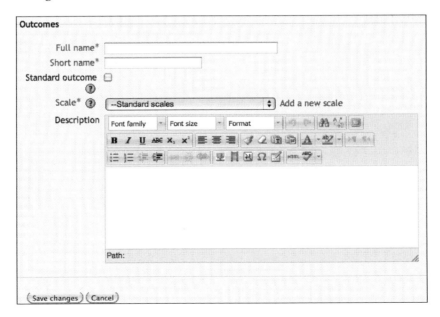

Administrators have the option of making the outcome a standard (sitewide) outcome by adding a tick to the **Standard outcome** box.

7. In the **Scale** drop-down box, choose the **Completion** scale we created earlier.

8. In the **Description** box, you can add more details of the outcome in case others use it (in this case, write "all evidence required has been submitted or seen by the teacher").

9. Click on **Save changes** at the bottom of the screen.

10. Repeat this process for the following two outcomes:

Full name and short name	Scale	Description
Criteria 2 met	**Completion**	All elements of criteria 2 have been met
Criteria 1 met	**Completion**	All elements of criteria 1 have been met

When you have saved changes for the final time, your custom outcomes screen should look as the following:

Custom outcomes				
Full name	Short name	Scale	Items	Edit
Criteria 1 met	Criteria 1 met	Completion	0	✎✗
Criteria 2 met	Criteria 2 met	Completion	0	✎✗
Evidence provided	Evidence provided	Completion	0	✎✗

(Add a new outcome) (Export all outcomes)

It is worth noting that outcomes can only be deleted before they are added to an assignment. Once used in an assignment, the delete option will not be available but you will still be able to edit. However, if the outcome is removed from all assignments, we will be able to delete the outcome from the course. We will look at how these outcomes are added to an assignment in *Chapter 3, Adding Graded Activities*.

Summary

Through the use of numerical grades, letter grades, and scales, a teacher can customize their gradebook to ensure it can meet the specific course requirements. Where required, a teacher can also make use of outcomes, which can be used in conjunction with a scale, to demonstrate competency against specific criteria. Each type of grade has its own benefits, but the options you would like for calculating the final grade should be considered before choosing your grade type to ensure it will meet your needs. Remember that the number grades, or grade letters can always be calculated more straightforwardly than word grades (scales). Scales should only be used when no grading or only simple grading is required. However, numerical grades and letter grades can be used for more complex grading requirements.

In the next chapter, we will take a look at how to add these grading options to assignments within Moodle before learning how to grade work.

3
Adding Graded Activities

In this chapter, we will look at how to add graded activities and set up grading for the assessments that will be graded, including choosing our custom scales and adding outcomes for grading. We will also see how to add additional graded items to the gradebook.

Adding assignments

All graded activities are added through the **Add an activity** drop-down list available within each topic or week within a Moodle course. We will use the assignments to explain how to add customized options to the graded activity. These instructions will not explain how to add each assignment, as we will concentrate on the options that are available to all graded activities rather than in assignments only.

For this example, we will use the offline assignment to look at the options available and how to choose them. The offline assignment allows teachers to add the assignment details and due date, but the student will not submit any work electronically. However, through adding the task details as an offline assignment, the teacher will be able to add the grade and feedback received, so that the student can review the information in the gradebook. For details of the other assignments available, please refer back to *Chapter 1, Introduction to the Gradebook*.

The area that we will be using within the assignment setup screen is the **Grade** section:

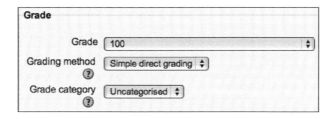

Let's work through the process to add the assignment and choose the grading options.

1. Make sure that editing is turned on for the course.
2. Click on **Add an activity**.
3. Click on **Assignments | Offline activity**.
4. In the **Assignment name** box, type in the name of the assignment (such as "assignment one").
5. In the **Description** box, provide the assignment details.
6. In the next box, you will see some options such as submission dates.
7. Go down to the **Grade** section (shown in the previous screenshot). This is where we can choose how we want to grade the assignment: we can choose to use numbers or a scale that we have created.

    ○   The default grade for all activities is 100. If a number grade is to be used, we need to choose the highest grade possible for this particular assignment. Click on the drop-down list (that currently has 100 in it) and a list of numbers will appear to choose the grade you would like to use.

    ○   If a scale is to be used instead, you will see the scale options at the top of the drop-down list (this will be above the numbers - you sometimes need to scroll up to see them). You can choose the scale you would like to use for this assignment.

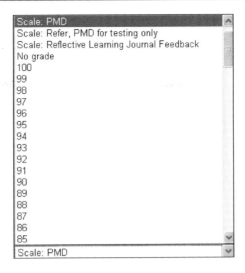

- ○ Choose the PMD scale that we set up in *Chapter 2, Customizing the Grades*.

- ○ You could also choose **No grade** if you would like to use the activity but not award a final grade (For example, when using the online text assignment for a reflective journal or blog, no grade will be given to the student for it).

8. Another option in this **Grade** section is the **Grading method**. There are two options: **Simple direct method** or **Rubric**. Keep this as the **Simple direct method**, as we will grade the work based on the grade we have chosen (for example, if 100 is chosen, we will be able to award a single grade between zero and 100. If a scale is chosen, we will be able to award one of the grades listed in that scale). We will look at the alternative rubric grading type later in the chapter.

9. A final option within the **Grade** section is the **Grade category**. Currently, the option in the drop-down list is uncategorized. This is the only option available until categories have been added within the **Grades** area. Categories enable graded activities to be grouped together within the gradebook. This will be explained in detail, with applied examples, in *Chapter 6, Organizing Using Categories*. However, once a category has been added to the course, it will appear in this drop-down list so that the graded activity can be organized and grouped within that category in the gradebook.

10. Scroll to the bottom of the screen and click on **Save and return to course**.

Remember, although we are using an assignment activity to look at these options, the **Grade** section is available in all graded activities (such as the quiz, lesson, forum, SCORM activities, and other activities with a grading option). All of these activities can be used with the **Simple direct method**, but some activities also allow you to use the **Rubric** grading method which will be explained later in the chapter.

Adding outcomes to an assignment

Another option we can add to a graded activity is outcomes, which can be graded with a scale along with adding a final grade for the assignment. In order to grade an outcome, the outcomes need to be added to the course.

In *Chapter 2, Customizing the Grades*, we created three outcomes and these can be added to any activity. Not all outcomes have to be added to all activities; different outcomes can be added to different activities. Let's have a go at adding some outcomes to an assignment.

1. Within a course where outcomes have been added, turn editing on and click on **Add an activity**.
2. Choose **Offline activity** (under the **Assignment** heading).
3. Give the assignment a name (for example, "task three").
4. In the **Description** box, give the assignment details.
5. In the **Grade** section, leave the **Grade** as **100** and the **Grading method** as **Simple direct grading**.
6. When outcomes have been created within the grades area of the course, an **Outcomes** section will be shown in the assignment setup screen.

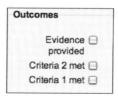

7. Choose two outcomes by clicking on the box next to them (choose **Evidence provided** and **Criteria 1 met**).
8. These two will then be assigned as the outcomes to meet for this assignment.
9. Scroll to the bottom of the screen and click on **Save and return to course**.

When we come to grade the assignment, we will now also have the option to grade the outcomes as well. We will do this in the next chapter.

We have seen how to customize and organize the graded activity to enable it to be used with the gradebook and to be awarded a grade. The **Simple direct method** of grading allows a single final grade to be awarded for the piece of work.

Advanced grading methods

Advanced grading methods are now available to enable individual elements of an assignment to be awarded a grade, and the final grade is calculated as a total of each of these grades. For example, the teacher grades element one and element two and the grades given will contribute to the final activity grade. The teacher will not choose one final grade for the assessment. This is achieved through the use of rubrics.

Rubrics

Rubrics are an advanced grading method. Until Moodle 2.2, advanced grading options have only been available in the **Workshop** activity, but the rubric option is now available for use with assignments as well.

Currently, Rubrics can only be used with assignment activities and as part of the **Workshop** activity. However, future releases of Moodle are likely to enable advanced grading methods to be used with other activities such as forums and glossaries.

Rubrics allow a set of criteria to be set up for the assessment along with descriptors to outline the different levels at which the criteria is met. Each descriptor has a value to enable Moodle to calculate a final grade for the assessment, based on the criteria met. This can be a more sophisticated way of grading work, while still making the grading process simple for the teacher and students.

When using the rubric grading method, we not only need to add the graded activity, but a grading form will also need to be created. We will set up a rubric assignment together.

1. Make sure that editing is turned on in the course.
2. Click on **Add an activity**.
3. Click on **Assignments | Upload a single file**.
4. In the **Assignment name** box, type in "assignment two".
5. In the **Description** box, type in the assignment details.
6. In the **Grade** section, change the **Grade** to **30** and change the **Grading method** to **Rubric**.

7. Scroll to the bottom of the screen and click on **Save and display**.

8. You will see the following advanced grading screen:

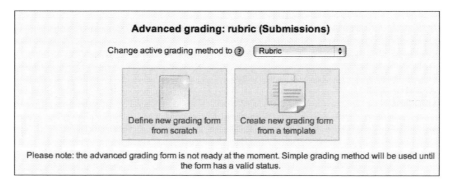

From this screen, we will define new grading form from scratch. However, note that you can also create a new grading form from a template. This enables you to use grading forms that you have already created in this or other courses, or use standard (sitewide) forms created on the Moodle site.

 If no rubric grading form is created at this stage, the assignment will make use of the standard **Simple direct grading** method when the work is assessed. This means the teacher will manually add in the final grade rather than grade using the criteria in a rubric. The red text under the grading form options highlights when the rubric is not ready.

As this is the first one we have created, click on **Define new grading form from scratch**. The following screen will appear:

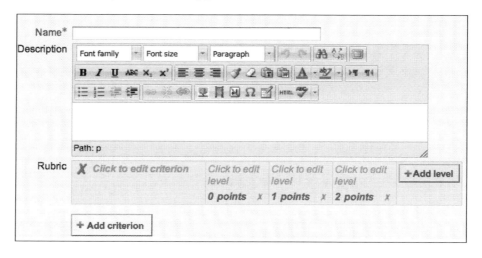

In the **Name** box, type in the name for this set of rubric criteria. For this example, we will call it "core assignment criteria". You can also add a **Description** into the box (this is useful when sharing rubrics or searching for your own rubrics to use as templates).

We will be completing the rubric criterion and level boxes, but first let's find out how rubrics are used and what these options are.

Within a rubric, there is at least one criterion, and each criterion has specific levels of grading. The criterion is an element of the assignment that needs to be met. The levels are the extent to which this criterion has been met. Statements can be provided, linked to the criterion, that can be used to assess the work and, when grading, we can choose the relevant statement based on the extent to which this criterion has been met. When marking work, the relevant level is selected and that is the number of points that are awarded as the final grade. For assignments with multiple criteria, the points awarded for each criterion are added together to create the final grade.

The default setting within a rubric is for one criterion with three points levels ranging from **0** to **2** points. We can add additional criterion as well as additional grading levels for each criterion (the number of grading levels can also be removed so that there can be fewer than three grading levels). The points awarded for each level can also be amended.

We will be setting up three criteria, each with a top grade of 10. If the student is graded the top marks for each of the three criteria, they will receive the top grade of 30 (we set 30 as the maximum grade when we added the assignment).

Please note, the criteria does not need to always add up to the maximum grade given for the assignment, as Moodle will convert the final grade received for the assignment (by adding together the grade awarded for each criterion) into a decimal and this will be multiplied by the maximum grade set for the assignment. This is a normalization process that is explained in much more detail in *Chapter 4, Assigning Grades*.

You can see the criteria we will be using in the following table. We will be using the same points system for each level in this example.

Criterion	0 points	3 points	6 points	10 points
The assignment should be 1000 words	The word count is below 800 words or over 1200 words	The word count is between 800 and 1049 words	The word count is between 1050 and 1200 words	The assignment is between 1000 and 1050
At least 5 quotes should be used and be correctly referenced	No quotes or quotes used but not referenced	Some quotes included but not fully referenced	5 quotes included and partly referenced	5 or more quotes included and correctly referenced
Assignment brief met (4 elements)	2 or fewer elements covered	3 elements covered	4 elements covered but more detail could be included	All 4 elements covered in detail

Let's add these criterion and levels to the course. We will do the first one together.

1. Click on the grey **Click to edit criterion** text (next to the red cross) to add the criteria detail.

2. Type in the first criterion (**The assignment should be 1000 words**). You can make the textbox larger by holding your arrow on the bottom right of the box and dragging the box to make it bigger.

3. Click on the grey **Click to edit level** text in the box to the right of the criterion we have just added. This is where we need to type the statement for the zero points level shown in the previous table (**The word count is below 800 words or over 1200 words**). Make sure the points box says **0**.

4. Click on the next grey **Click to edit level** text in the box (currently the **1** points level). Type in the three points level statement from the table. Change the points number to **3**.

5. Click on the last available level box and add in the six points statement and change the number of points to **6**.

6. We have now run out of the default number of levels but we still need somewhere to add the ten points level. Click on the **+ Add level** button on the right-hand side of the current level we are working on.

7. Add in the level statement for 10 points and change the points to **10**.

8. Click anywhere on the screen to finalize this text.

9. We now need to add another line for the next criterion. Under the current criterion, there is a button saying **+ Add criterion**. Click on this and an additional row will appear to add another criterion and the level statements and points. Use the previous table to complete this rubric.

10. Once completed, your rubric table should look like this:

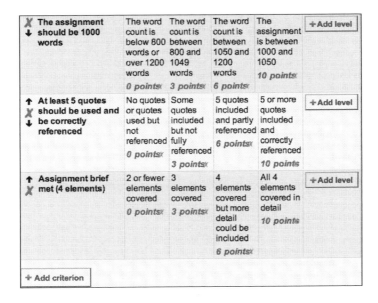

11. Scroll to the bottom of the screen and click on **Save rubric and make it ready**.

Your rubric is now ready and your screen will look like this:

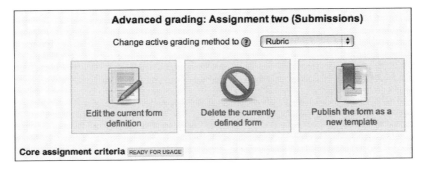

You can see the rubric is now ready for use (as shown at the bottom of the screenshot). You can still edit the rubric criteria and levels, or you can delete it (to start a new form or to revert to the **Simple direct grading** method). You can also publish this form, so that it can be used by others.

If you want to stop working in the rubric before it is complete, you can save it as a draft to come back to later. If you do this, the previous screenshot will say **DRAFT** rather than **READY FOR USAGE**, so that you know it is not yet complete.

The rubric is now ready for use when grading work. We will look at how to grade this in the next chapter.

If you want to edit your rubric, you will not see the **Advanced grading**. However, you can still access the Rubric screen by using the **Settings** block when you are viewing the assignment on the screen. Click on **Advanced grading** and then choose **Define rubric**, which will take you into the Rubric editing screen.

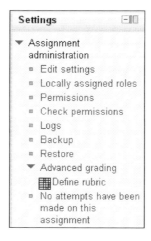

Adding additional grades directly into the gradebook

We have looked at how we can add graded activities to a Moodle course so that they can be awarded a mark and used with the gradebook. This is the main way in which we grade work as the students need to complete something to be graded (whether this is an assignment, quiz, discussion, or other Moodle activity). With the offline assignment type, it is possible to have an activity on the Moodle course where there is no requirement for the student to complete any work online but still allows us to provide feedback and grades on activities such as class presentations or practical work.

However, what if you would like a grade to be added to the gradebook that is not linked to any activities? Perhaps students receive an additional grade based on their attendance in lessons. You may want the grade to be calculated within the gradebook for the final course grade, but you do not want it to appear as an activity within the Moodle course. This is where a **Graded item**, added directly into the Moodle gradebook, could be useful.

1. From the main course screen, find the **Settings** block and click on **Grades** to get to the gradebook.

2. Go into the **Categories and items** screen (click on the **Categories and items** tab at the top of the **Grades** page, if the tabs are available. Otherwise, click on the drop-down list and click on **Simple view** under the **Categories and items** heading).

3. At the bottom of the screen, click on **Add grade item**. The following screen will appear:

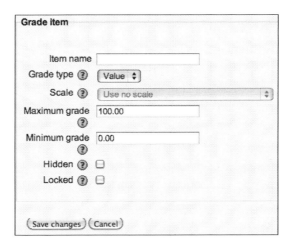

4. Give the graded item a name (using the previous example, we could call this "attendance grade").

5. There are four Grade types available for graded items:
    ° **Value** enables a number grade to be awarded. If this is used, the maximum and minimum grades possible can be set.
    ° **Scale** allows you to choose a scale that is available within the course, to grade this item. If this is chosen, the scale drop-down list becomes available to enable us to choose the scale we would like to use.
    ° **Text** does not allow any grade to be used but written feedback can be added. This will not be used in gradebook calculations.
    ° **None** means that no grade is assigned to this item.

6. For this example, we will use **Value** and keep the default maximum (**100.00**) and minimum (**0.00**) grades as shown on the screen.

7. Click on **Save changes**.

Summary

In this chapter, we have added two different assignment types as examples of graded activities. We have also chosen the grading method, including choosing scales and outcomes as created in the previous chapter. We have also added a rubric and seen how to add additional levels and criteria to it, as required. Finally, we saw how to add a new graded item into the gradebook.

In the next chapter, we will look at grading assessments. We will add number and scale grades, written feedback, grade outcomes, and grade an assignment using the rubric we have just created.

4
Assigning Grades

In the previous chapter we added two assignments, one using a scale and one making use of outcomes. We also created a rubric for advanced grading before finally adding a graded item directly into the gradebook.

Once the graded activities are added to a Moodle course, we need to award grades to the students. Some of the activities are graded by Moodle, such as quizzes and some elements of lessons, but those with a lot of written content need to be reviewed and graded by the teacher.

In this chapter, we will look at different ways of grading work, in particular assignments, that have been set up with different types of grades. We will see how to:

- Grade assignments with number grades, scales, outcomes, and rubrics
- View electronically submitted assignments
- Add written feedback
- Use quick grading directly within the gradebook

Grading an assignment

Let's first find our way to the assignments and the grading screen:

1. Within the course, click on the name of the assignment that you would like to grade. This will take you to the assignment details screen that has already been set up to provide the assessment information to the students.

2. Within the assignment screen, the top-right area will have a link to the grading area. Where no files have been uploaded, the text will say **View assignment grades and feedback**. If work has been uploaded or written online, the text at the top-right of the screen will show the number of submitted assignments: **View** *(number)* **submitted assignments**.

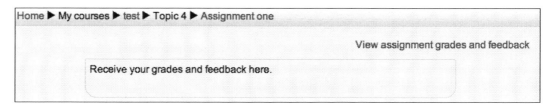

3. Click on this link to go to the assignment grading area.

The grading screen will look like this:

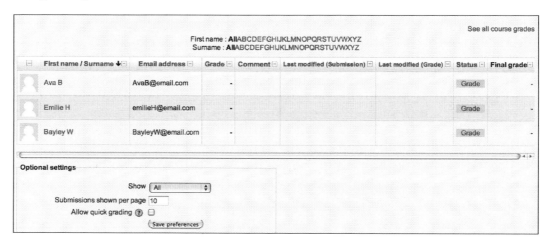

There is a lot of information on this screen, so we will look at each individual section. The first area we are going to use is in the central table, which has the name of each student on the left and a **Grade** button on each student row. This is where we will access the grading screen for the individual student.

The following screenshot shows an assessment area for an assignment where the student has submitted work. The **Last modified (Submission)** column has information within it to show that one or more files have been uploaded, and the date and time at which this happened.

We can use the headings to sort the contents of the table. For example, clicking on the **Last modified (Submission)** column will put the students in order so that those who have not submitted work will appear at the top and those who have submitted work will appear at the bottom. Click on this column heading again and all the students with submitted work will appear at the top of the list. This is very useful when grading work. Similarly, you can change the order based on whether work has been graded yet by using the **Status** column.

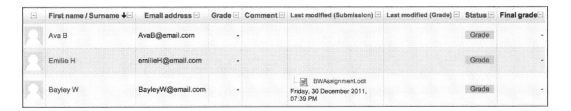

	First name / Surname ↓	Email address	Grade	Comment	Last modified (Submission)	Last modified (Grade)	Status	Final grade
	Ava B	AvaB@email.com	-				Grade	-
	Emilie H	emilieH@email.com	-				Grade	-
	Bayley W	BayleyW@email.com	-		BWAssignment.odt Friday, 30 December 2011, 07:39 PM		Grade	-

Click on the **Grade** button, in the **Status** column, next to the student you want to grade. There are three main sections to the individual grading screen. We will look at each one in turn.

The Submission section

The **Submission** section shows any work that has been submitted by the student (either uploaded files or written text in the case of an online text assignment). It will not have any information in it if it is an offline activity assignment type.

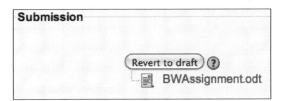

When files are uploaded, the teacher can click on them to open them to view the content. This opens within the relevant software, so it can be open in one window while the teacher adds written feedback into Moodle in another window.

If the work submitted does not meet the requirements and the student is able to resubmit the work, the teacher can use the **Revert to draft** button to enable the student to upload a new version.

The **Revert to draft** button will refresh the individual grading screen so any other work completed (such as the grade and feedback) will be lost. Hence, this button should be pressed before any other work is completed.

The Grades section

The following screenshot shows the **Grades** section and provides us with the option of choosing and presenting the grade for the piece of work.

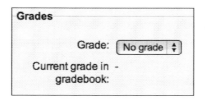

The **Grade** drop-down list will have the options available based on the grading scale or maximum score that was chosen when the assignment was initially created. When grading this assignment for the first time, the current grade will always be **No grade**. If re-grading the work, the **Current grade in gradebook** will show the previous grade awarded for this piece of work.

If a number grade was used, each number from zero to the maximum grade available will be shown in the list. In the previous example, the maximum grade is 100, so it will be a long list of options. The teacher will choose the grade that they would like to award and that will be shown as the final grade.

```
12 / 100
11 / 100
10 / 100
 9 / 100
 8 / 100
 7 / 100
 6 / 100
 5 / 100
 4 / 100
 3 / 100
 2 / 100
 1 / 100
 0 / 100
✓ No grade
```

If a scale is used, all the options for the scale are shown in the grade list. The teacher clicks on the grade that they would like to award.

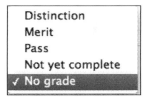

The Feedback section

This is the section where written feedback can be provided for the students.

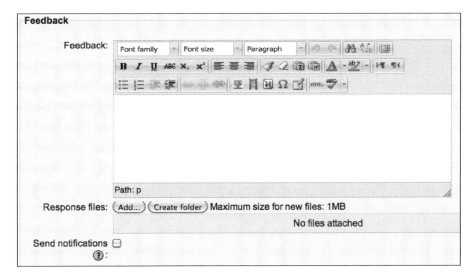

The **Feedback** area has an editing toolbar to enable the teacher to change how the feedback appears. In addition to the standard editing and formatting features, there is a useful spellcheck tool and a toggle fullscreen option to use the full window for writing feedback. Holding your mouse over an icon on the toolbar will provide you with a tool tip to show its function. There is also a resizing option at the bottom right-hand corner of the feedback box, if more space is required.

The **Response files** option is only shown in the advanced uploading of files assignment type, but it allows the teacher or assessor to upload additional files to be attached to the assignment feedback if required. This could be a more detailed feedback in a specific format or template, audio feedback (such as an audio MP3 recording), or other resources that may be useful for the individual student.

The **Send notifications** option is available within all assignment types. Clicking on the box next to this text will send a notification to the student when the assignment has been graded and saved by the teacher (by default, this will normally be an e-mail, but individual students can change how this notification is received).

Once each of these sections has been completed, the grade information and feedback can be saved so that further grading can take place or to finish grading. There are four options at the bottom of the individual grading screen.

- **Save changes**: This enables you to save the grade and feedback, and return to the assignment grading area.

- **Save and show next**: This will save the grade and feedback and move onto the next individual grading page to grade another assignment. Teachers will work through the students in the order in which the assignment screen has been sorted. By default, this will usually be alphabetical by name, but a teacher can change the order by clicking on a column heading to sort the information based on the content of that column. The final student to be graded will not have a **Save and show next** option on their individual grading screen.

- **Next**: This will move onto the next individual grading page but will not save any work completed on the current grading screen.

- **Cancel**: This will cancel any work completed on the current individual grading screen and will show the assignment grading area.

Once the grading has been completed, you will see that the grading area is also updated. Take a look at **Bayley W** in the following screenshot:

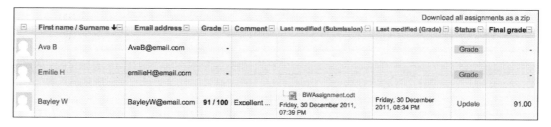

A grade is now shown in the **Grade** column and you can see the beginning of the written feedback provided (holding your mouse over a grade at any time will also show you a small amount of the written feedback). As well as the **Last modified (Submission)** column showing when the student submitted the work (remember that nothing will appear here for offline activities), there is now some information in the **Last modified (Grade)** column, which is the most recent time and date when the individual grading screen was reviewed, or amended, and saved by the teacher. In the **Status** column, **Bayley W** has an **Update** link rather than a **Grade** button, which indicates that the teacher was the last person to do anything for this particular assignment.

If **Allow resubmitting** has been set to **Yes** when the assignment was created and a student resubmits their work, the **Last modified (Submission)** column will have an updated date and the **Status** column will revert to a **Grade** button.

 Notice above the **Status** and **Final grade** columns that there is the option to **Download all assignments as a zip**. This allows teachers to download all of the uploaded files into a single ZIP file to enable the work to be reviewed offline.

The process for grading is the same for all assignment types, although additional plugins or uploaded file assignment types may have additional options to enhance the feedback that can be provided. This information is automatically included in the gradebook.

We will will look at grading outcomes and rubrics later, but let's first look at some of the other options on the assignment grading screen. In particular, let's look at the **Optional settings**.

The Optional settings section

Individual teachers can customize how they view the assignment grading area. There are three main options shown at the bottom of the assignment grading screen, within the **Optional settings**:

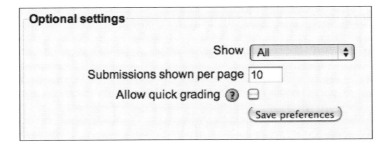

The **Show** option allows the teacher to choose what to view on the screen. The default is **All**, but there are two other options:

- **Require grading**: This will only show work that needs to be graded. In the case of assignments, where work needs to be uploaded or written online, this will only show the students where assignments have been submitted and need grading (where the **Status** column states **Grade** rather than **Update**). For the offline activity, this will show all assignments that need to be graded.

- **Submitted**: This will show all students where work has been submitted, regardless of whether it has been graded or not.

The **Submissions shown per page** option, currently set to **10**, allows the teacher to choose how many students can be shown per page. For example, if we have 12 students on the course, we can choose to view all 12 on one screen rather than moving to another screen to review the final two students. Alternatively, if the students are submitting many files per assignment, we may only want to view one or two students per page so that we can see all the information easily on the screen.

The final option is **Allow quick grading**. A tick in this box will give us an alternative way to grade the students' work. Put a tick into this box and click on **Save preferences** and we will see what it does!

Quick grading within the grading screen

Quick grading enables us to add a grade and some written feedback directly from the assignment grading area.

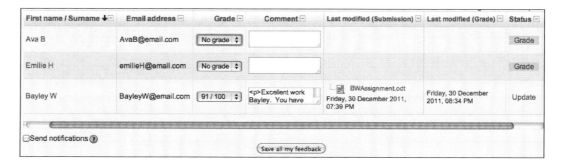

The **Grade** column now has a drop-down list, next to each student, to enable the teacher to choose the grade that they would like to award. This is the same drop-down list as on the individual grading screen and will show the number or the scale grade as before.

There is also a small area in the **Comment** column to enable written feedback to be provided. The feedback box can be made larger with the resizing area in the bottom-right of the box, but there is no editor to change how the information looks.

Quick grading still allows the teacher to open the submitted files from within the **Last modified (Submission)** column, but it does not allow us to attach files as feedback.

Once all the grades and written feedback have been added, it is important to click on **Save all my feedback** in order to save the work completed.

Quick feedback is very useful for offline activities where the work has already been reviewed offline, or for assessments where only grades or short comments are required.

Other options when using the assignment grading table

The assignment grading table can become quite long when it has a lot of information in it. Some columns may not need to be viewed all the time, so that individual users can customize how they see these columns.

Next to the heading at the top of each column, there is a – symbol. Clicking on this will collapse this column and hide the contents to enable more space on the screen for the rest of the table. You can collapse as many columns as you want. Once collapsed, a + symbol appears instead, to enable you to expand and view the contents again.

These changes will be seen for the individual user on all assignment screens, but it can be amended on any assignment screen.

Grading an assignment with outcomes

Along with the assignments with number and scale grades, we also set up an assignment that made use of outcomes. When using outcomes, there are additional areas to assess achievement.

On the assignment grading screen, the only difference is the addition of an **Outcome** column at the end of the grades table.

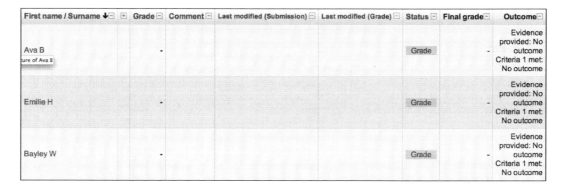

We will use the individual grading screen to grade the outcomes, so we need to click on **Grade**, next to the student whose work we want to mark.

The **Grades** section has an additional **Grade** drop-down list for each outcome that is assigned to the assignment.

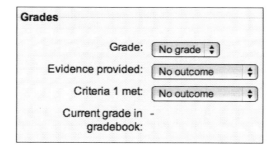

A final grade is still awarded if a grade was set up with the assignment. In the previous example, there is a maximum final grade of 100.

However, there are additional items to grade now. The name of the outcome is listed on the left and the drop-down list will have the scale options that were chosen when the outcomes were created. To assign a grade, the process is the same as for the main grade: simply choose the option required from the drop-down list.

The rest of the grading process is the same as previously and the outcome grades will be shown in the **Outcome** column, within the assignment grading area.

Grading an assignment with a rubric

In *Chapter 3, Adding Graded Activities*, we created an assignment that used the advanced grading methods, and we also created a rubric grading profile. As with grading outcomes, previously explained, the only element that is different when using the individual grading screen for a rubric-graded assignment is the **Grades** section. However, within rubric grading there is no **Grades** drop-down list. Instead, there is a table that enables specific criterion to be graded.

Grades						
Grade:	The assignment should be 1000 words *0 points*	The word count is below 800 words or over 1200 words *3 points*	The word count is between 800 and 1049 words *6 points*	The word count is between 1050 and 1200 words *10 points*	The assignment is between 1000 and 1050	
	At least 5 quotes should be used and be correctly referenced	No quotes or quotes used but not referenced *0 points*	Some quotes included but not fully referenced *3 points*	5 quotes included and partly referenced *6 points*	5 or more quotes included and correctly referenced *10 points*	
	Assignment brief met (4 elements)	2 or fewer elements covered *0 points*	3 elements covered *3 points*	4 elements covered but more detail could be included *6 points*	All 4 elements covered in detail *10 points*	

You can see the rubric criteria and levels in the previous screenshot. The table enables us to easily grade work even though there is a lot of information on the screen.

When grading, the teacher reviews the work and simply clicks on the box that contains the statement and points that they want to award.

At the right-hand side of the row that contains the criteria, there is a textbox to enable additional comments to be made. However, the main assignment feedback screen is still available on the individual assignment screen (the rubric grid is shown in the following screenshot).

You can see in the following grid how this rubric grid has been completed by the teacher:

Grade:	The assignment should be 1000 words *0 points*	The word count is below 800 words or over 1200 words *3 points*	The word count is between 800 and 1049 words *6 points*	The word count is between 1050 and 1200 words *10 points*	The assignment is between 1000 and 1050	Word count: 1119
	At least 5 quotes should be used and be correctly referenced	No quotes or quotes used but not referenced *0 points*	Some quotes included but not fully referenced *3 points*	5 quotes included and partly referenced *6 points*	5 or more quotes included and correctly referenced *10 points*	You need to check your referencing and update your work.
	Assignment brief met (4 elements)	2 or fewer elements covered *0 points*	3 elements covered *3 points*	4 elements covered but more detail could be included *6 points*	All 4 elements covered in detail *10 points*	Excellent work.

The shaded boxes show the grade awarded for each criterion and some comments have been added to the feedback column.

The **Final grade** for the assignment is calculated by Moodle, by adding together each of the points awarded within the rubric. This final grade is only shown in the assignment grading area in the **Grade** and **Final Grade** columns, as shown in the following screenshot for **Ava B**:

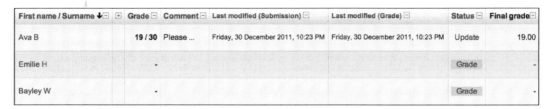

First name / Surname ↓		Grade	Comment	Last modified (Submission)	Last modified (Grade)	Status	Final grade
Ava B		19 / 30	Please ...	Friday, 30 December 2011, 10:23 PM	Friday, 30 December 2011, 10:23 PM	Update	19.00
Emilie H		-				Grade	-
Bayley W		-				Grade	-

The student will see the full rubric table and comments when they receive their assignment feedback.

Grading a graded item within the gradebook

We have seen how we can grade assignments by accessing the activities from within the main course screen. However, in *Chapter 3, Adding Graded Activities* , we also added a graded activity directly into the gradebook. So how do we grade this? We go into the gradebook!

1. From the main course screen, go to the **Grades** area (click on **Settings | Grades**).

2. Click on **Turn editing on** in the top-right corner of the screen.

3. We will be able to add a grade directly into the graded item.

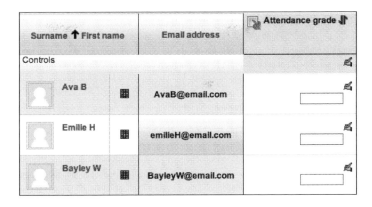

In the previous screenshot, you can see the **Attendance grade** item we added earlier. As this item was set up as a value grade, we can simply type in the grade we want to award. At the bottom of the screen, there is an **Update** button to save any grades we have added.

We can also use this grading method for any other type of graded activity within the gradebook.

Quick grading within the gradebook

As in the graded item, turning editing on within the **Grades** area will allow us to grade any graded activity.

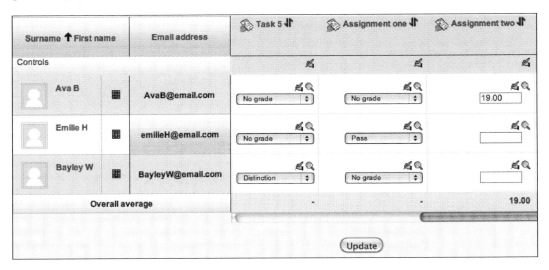

In the previous screenshot, we can see two different types of grades. **Task 5** and **Assignment one** are both examples of assignments that are graded with a scale, and therefore quick grading provides a drop-down list to enable the teacher to choose the grade they would like to award. **Assignment two**, however, has been set as a numerical scale, so we need to type the number indicating the grade awarded directly into the empty box.

There are a few things to consider when using quick grading:

- We cannot see the maximum grade when adding number grades
- Rubric graded assignments cannot be marked through the quick grading option (but outcomes can be graded through quick grading)

When using the quick grading within the assignment area, we can add quick feedback as well, but this option is not shown on the current screen. However, we can change a setting to enable this:

1. Click on the **My preferences** tab within the grader view or use the drop-down list and click on **Grader report** under the **My preferences** heading.
2. Scroll to the bottom of the page to the **General** section.
3. Next to the **Show quick feedback text**, change the drop-down list to **Yes**.
4. Click on **Save changes** at the bottom of the page.

As before, the quick feedback option is limited for adding text. So, if a lot of text is required, it is recommended that the individual grading screen is used.

Summary

In this chapter, we have seen how to grade assignments that have number or scale grades, graded outcomes, and we have used the rubric grading form. We have also seen how we can use the quick grading options within the assignment area and the gradebook screen.

We have seen how we can grade individual assignments, but how do these all come together in the gradebook? In the next chapter, we will look at how the grades can work together in the gradebook, and how calculations can be set up to calculate final course grades. We will also see how we can further customize the gradebook.

5
Using Calculations

In this chapter, you will learn about the various options and settings available to calculate and display a final grade in the gradebook. We will also look at the options available for choosing how the grades are displayed. In this chapter, we will:

- See how grades are calculated
- Use a range of preset aggregations to calculate course totals
- Change how grades are shown in the gradebook

Calculating the course grade

All graded activities that are added to the online course will automatically be added to the gradebook. The students can have a range of assessments for which they will be given a range of scores. Apart from storing these grades, the gradebook can also calculate a final grade based on a range of preset aggregation settings available within the course. **Aggregation** is bringing together all the scores and then doing a calculation to present a final score.

Before this aggregation takes place, a normalization process occurs. **Normalization** is when the grade given to an individual assessment is converted into a percentage and then used as a decimal for the calculations.

Why use normalization?

Normalization is necessary to ensure that all the grades have the same base value so that they can be calculated fairly in relation to the maximum grade. For example, a grade of 20 out of 100 is a lower percentage score than 20 out of 20. So, using both scores as 20 would not represent the achievement by the learner.

In order for the gradebook to calculate a fair total, we need both of the grades to be recalculated into a decimal so that they have the same base value prior to adding them together for the final course grade. The calculation for normalization is the grade awarded divided by the total grade possible, so that all the graded activities have a base value of 10. The following table shows this for the two activities in this example:

	Graded activity 1	Graded activity 2
Maximum grade possible	20	100
Grade awarded	20	20
Grade following normalization	1.0	0.2

As you can see, the normalized grade now shows that the two awarded scores of 20 should not be treated the same when calculating the final course grade, as they have significantly different decimal scores. It is this score that is used in the aggregation process.

We will see many more examples of how this normalization process is used as we complete examples throughout the chapter and see how the different aggregation types use the normalized grades.

Aggregation types

Moodle has a range of aggregation types available and these are outlined briefly as follows. These are shown in the order they are listed within Moodle. The ones shown in bold, which are some of the most popular or the more complex to understand, will be used as detailed examples later in the chapter, and the actual calculations will be explained in more detail. However, for each of the following aggregation types, quick examples will also be given to show the calculation that takes place. For all the examples, the normalized grades of 1.0 and 0.2, as shown in the previous example, will be used.

- **Mean of grades**: Following normalization, the average score is calculated as the final score by adding up the total grades awarded and dividing it by the total number of graded items. Quick example: (1.0 + 0.2)/2=0.6.

- **Weighted mean of grades**: Each graded item can be given a weight. The grade given for the assessed item is normalized and then multiplied by the item's weight to create an increased item grade. The final grade is calculated by adding together the increased item grades and then dividing this by the total weights applied (for example, if two assessments are given a x2 weight, the total of the increased grades added together will be divided by four).

Quick example: (using a weighting of x2 for graded item one, and x3 for graded item two): (1.0x2)+(0.2x3)/5=0.52.

- **Simple weighted mean of grades**: In this version of the weighted mean type, the maximum grades of each assessed item are used as the weighting, instead of the teacher needing to apply separate weights to each graded activity. For example, one assessed activity could be graded out of 100 and another activity could be graded out of 50. The first graded item would be worth more to the final course total than the second. Again, the gradebook first normalizes the grade and then multiplies that grade by the total grade possible. These increased assessment activity grades are then divided by the total weight possible (that is, the total of all the maximum grades in the course). Quick example: (1.0x20)+(0.2x100)/120=0.333.

- Mean of grades (with extra credit): This aggregation type is only available in Moodle to enable upgraded courses that already use this aggregation type to continue to use it (that is, for backwards compatibility). The weighted and simple weighted means options should be used instead to prevent the use of an aggregation method that is no longer supported.

- Median of grades: All the normalized grades are put into numerical order from lowest to the highest, and the final grade will be the grade in the middle of this list. If there is no middle number (if the total number of grades is an even number), Moodle will take the two middle numbers and present the average grade of these two as the final grade. Quick example: As there are only two numbers in our example, the final course grade will be an average - (1.0+02)/2=0.6. To show as an example, an additional graded item will be included. This grade will be 30 out of 30 which will provide a normalized grade of 1.0. Therefore, there are now three grades for this example: 0.2. 1.0 and 1.0 which are shown in order from lowest to highest. The gradebook will present the final grade as 1.0 as this is the grade in the middle.

- **Lowest grade**: Reviews all the grades, after normalization, and presents the lowest score as the final grade. Quick example: The final grade will be 0.2.

- Highest grade: Reviews all the grades, after normalization, and presents the highest score as the final grade. Quick example: The final grade will be 1.0.

- Mode of grades: Following normalization, the gradebook reviews all the grades and the grade that is awarded most frequently is presented as the final grade. Quick example: 0.2, 1.0, and 1.0. Final grade = 1.0.

- **Sum of grades**: This is the only aggregation method that does not use normalization. In this aggregation type, the gradebook simply adds together each score awarded for each assessment. This maximum grade possible for the course is all the maximum grades possible for each individual assessment added together. Quick example: 20 + 20 = 40 out of a maximum grade of 120.

Maximum grades

It is possible to set a maximum score for the course which means that Moodle will calculate the final score based on that maximum grade.

For example, ten assessments in a course, each with a maximum grade of 25, will have a course total of 250. However, the final course grade achievable may only be 100. Therefore, the aggregation process can also convert the final score so that it is graded out of 100 (rather than 250).

Where a maximum score is applied, the gradebook will add an additional calculation after aggregation as shown in the following step 3. Therefore, the full aggregation process will be:

1. Normalize grades.
2. Aggregation calculation (for example, apply weights, add grades together, calculate average, and so on).
3. Multiply the aggregated normalized grades by the course maximum grade.

 Maximum grades do not apply with the sum of grades aggregation.

Confused? Let's take a look at an example to see the normalization, aggregation, and maximum grade calculations in action! Take a look at the following table and note the formulas shown in brackets to see the processes that the gradebook is completing for us.

In this example, there are five graded activities within the course, each with a different maximum grade possible. The gradebook aggregation is set as a mean of grades calculation (the average of the grades). The maximum grade possible for the whole course is 100. The shaded row is the information that the gradebook uses for the aggregation/calculations.

Assignment	A1	A2	A3	A4	A5	Usual total	Mean aggregation	Final grade shown in gradebook
Max grade possible	25	50	40	25	20	160	32	
Grade awarded	20	35	38	25	15	133	26.6	
Normalized grade	0.8	0.7	0.95	1	0.75	4.2	0.84	84
	(20/25)	(35/50)	(38/40)	(25/25)	(15/20)	(.8+.7+.95+ 1+.75)	(4.2/5)	(.84*100)

To calculate the normalized grade, the grade awarded is divided by the maximum grade for each assignment. The calculation used is shown in brackets in the shaded row for columns A1 to A5.

The mean aggregation grade is calculated by adding together the normalized grade for each of the grade items (the calculation is shown in the shaded row for the column Usual total). This is then divided by the total number of grades awarded which, in this example, is 5. This calculation is shown in the shaded row in the Mean aggregation column.

The final grade is 84. The mean aggregation grade is multiplied by 100 which is the course maximum (you can see the calculation in the Final grade shown in the gradebook column). If the course maximum was 30, the final grade would have been 25.2 (0.84*30=25.2).

Let's go into the gradebook and set up some examples to see the aggregation types in action, and learn some other things that we can do to customize the gradebook so that it can further meet our needs.

Example one – mean of grades

In this example, three assignments have been added to the Moodle course. Two have a maximum grade of 100 and one has a final grade of 50. If you would like to follow the instructions to set up an example gradebook, create three assignments (the type doesn't matter) and choose 100 for the maximum grade for **Task 1** and **Task 2**, and 50 for **Task 3**. Grade **Tasks 1** and **Task 2** for at least one learner. You can see the example that we will use for the activities in the following screenshot:

Surname ↑ First name		Email address	Task 1	Task 2	Task 3
Ava B		AvaB@email.com	94.00	-	-
Emilie H		emilieH@email.com	99.00	-	-
Bayley W		BayleyW@email.com	91.00	100.00	-
Overall average			94.67	100.00	-

The aggregation type of this course will be mean of grades which will present a final average grade.

Let's go into the grades area and choose the aggregation type.

Click on the **Settings** block and click on **Grades**. You should see a table, as shown in the previous screenshot, showing the grades of each assignment for each student. (If you see an **Overall average** row at the bottom of the screen, don't let this confuse you. This is an average grade based on all the students in the course rather than an individual students average grade, and it is shown for all aggregation types. You will learn more about customizing this screen in *Chapter 7, Reporting with the Gradebook*.)

From the drop-down list at the top of the screen, find **Categories and items** and choose **Simple view** (or click on the **Categories and items** tab, if your screen shows the tabs view).

This is where we can start to customize the gradebook and choose the aggregation type.

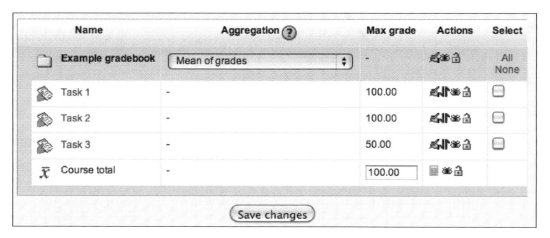

You can see that the **Categories and items** screen is another table with column headings explaining the content of the table. You can change the aggregation of the course from the drop-down list in the aggregation column. Click on the drop-down list box and choose **Mean of grades** and then click on **Save changes** at the bottom of the screen. This is not the only way to change the aggregation type; we will look at other ways of doing this later in the chapter.

Take a look at the **Max grade** column. This shows the maximum grade possible for each graded item in the course; and the **Course total**, the number at the bottom of the table, shows the total final grade possible. In this example, it is showing as **100.00**, as this is the default (except for the sum of grades aggregation type), but it can be easily changed by typing an alternative number into this course total box.

Let's switch back to view the gradebook. On the drop-down list at the top of the screen, find **View** and click on **Grader report** (or click on **View** on the tab at the top of the gradebook screen).

Before we look at other customizations possible, let's take a quick look at how the aggregation will work in this example. Remember, for this example we are using the mean of grades aggregation type and this type of calculation converts the grades to a normalized score, adds them all together, and divides this normalized total by the total number of graded items in the course. Finally, this is multiplied by the course total, in this case 100, to provide the final score.

Take a look at the following screenshot and you can see the **Course total** which is showing the mean grade for each student.

			Task 1	Task 2	Task 3	Course total
Surname ↑ First name		Email address				
Ava B		AvaB@email.com	94.00	-	-	94.00
Emilie H		emilieH@email.com	99.00	-	-	99.00
Bayley W		BayleyW@email.com	91.00	100.00	-	95.50
Overall average			94.67	100.00	-	96.17

Take a look at **Bayley W** who has completed two assessments which have been graded. His current course total is **95.50** which could be the following calculation: 91.00 + 100.00 / 2 (that is, the two assignment grades added together and divided by the total number of grades added together). However, this only works because the course total is the same as the assignment maximum grades. If the course total was 50, we could not do this simple calculation for the course total. This is why Moodle normalizes grades first and then multiplies this by the maximum course total possible. So, the calculation that Moodle is actually doing for **Bayley W** is shown as follows:

	Task 1	Task 2	Total	Mean aggregation	Final grade shown in gradebook
Max grade possible	100	100			
Grade awarded	91.00	100.00	191	95.50	
Normalized grade	0.91	1	1.91	0.955	95.50
	(91/100)	(100/100)	(0.91+1)	(1.91/2)	(.0955*100)

Using Calculations

As you can see, only the assessments that have actually been graded are included in the aggregation for the course total. So the student is given a current grade, based on work already completed. But, what if you want to provide a running total? What if you want the students to know the final grade they will get based on the work completed to date, even if it is not all yet completed? This is particularly important if all work needs to be completed in order to complete the course and gain a final grade.

Including all graded activities

We can tell the gradebook to include all the graded activities in the aggregation. Moodle will add up each assessed activity, which will include a zero score for each assessed item which has not yet been submitted or graded, and divide by the total number of assessed grades in the course, regardless of whether they have been graded or not. In this example, it will be divided by three. Let's go and apply this and see it in action!

- Go into **Categories and items** again (either by clicking on the drop-down list and clicking on **Simple view** under the **Categories and items** heading, or by clicking on **Categories and items** on the tabs bar).

- On the top row in the **Actions** column (on the same row as the aggregation drop-down list) the first icon is an edit icon (a hand and pen for the default Moodle theme, but it can also be shown as a spanner in some themes. If you hold your mouse over the first icon, it will give you a screen tip that says **Edit**). Click on the edit icon.

You will see this screen.

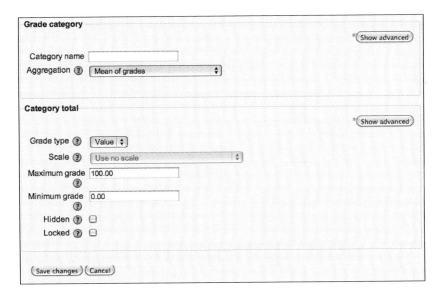

We are only going to use the **Grade category** section for now (we will be using the **Category total** section later). However, we need the advanced options, so click on the **Show advanced** button on the top-right of the screen.

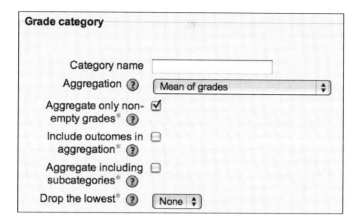

Note that you can change the aggregation method on this screen. However, the setting we need to change is the **Aggregate only non-empty grades** option. Notice that there is currently a tick in this box. Click on the box to remove the tick and scroll to the bottom of the screen to **Save changes**.

 This advanced setting can be applied with any aggregation type (except sum of grades) by clicking on the edit icon in the **Actions** column on the **Categories and items** screen.

Let's take a look at the gradebook again to see what difference this has made. (To go back to the gradebook, use the drop-down list at the top of the screen, find **View** and click on **Grader report** or click on **View** on the tab at the top of the gradebook screen).

Surname ↑ First name			Email address	🗞 Task 1 ↓↑	🗞 Task 2 ↓↑	🗞 Task 3 ↓↑	x̄ Course total ↓↑
	Ava B	▦	AvaB@email.com	94.00 🔍	- 🔍	- 🔍	31.33
	Emilie H	▦	emilieH@email.com	99.00 🔍	- 🔍	- 🔍	33.00
	Bayley W	▦	BayleyW@email.com	91.00 🔍	100.00 🔍	- 🔍	63.67
Overall average				94.67	100.00	-	42.67

You can see that the course total has now changed, as it is including all the graded items in the aggregation. The fewer the items that have been marked, the lower the grade will be. The calculation that is taking place for Bayley W is as follows:

	Task 1	Task 2	Task 3	Total	Mean aggregation	Final grade shown in gradebook
Max grade possible	100	100	50			
Grade awarded	91.00	100.00	0	191	63.67	
Normalized grade	0.91	1	0	1.91	0.6367	63.67
	(91/100)	(100/100)	(0/50)	(0.91+1+0)	(1.91/3)	(.06367*100)

We have been using mean of grades, but there are two other mean aggregation types.

Let's keep using this example, but change the gradebook to show the **Simple weighted mean of grades** and the **Weighted mean of grades** to see how they affect the final aggregation. It will also give us the chance to practice changing aggregation types within the course.

Simple weighted mean of grades

In the mean of grades aggregation type that we have been using, the totals for each assignment type are not taken into consideration in the final aggregation (other than for the normalization process). It is only the grades that are used. However, in the simple weighted mean of grades aggregation type, the maximum grade of each assignment is very important. This aggregation type uses the assignment totals in the mean aggregation step of the calculation.

Let's change the aggregation of the course and see what it does to the final grade.

- Go to **Categories and items** again (either by clicking on the drop-down list and clicking on **Simple view** under the **Categories and items** heading, or by clicking on **Categories and items** on the tabs bar).

- Change the aggregation type to **Simple weighted mean of grades** with the drop-down list in the aggregation column and click on **Save changes** at the bottom of the screen.

- Now, switch back to view the gradebook. On the drop-down list at the top of the screen, find **View** and click on **Grader report** (or click on **View** on the tab at the top of the gradebook screen).

Note how the course total score has changed. Look at **Bayley W** again. His previous score in the mean of grades aggregation was 63.67 (remember, that the gradebook is currently using *ALL* the assessed activities in the calculations, not just those that have been marked and graded). It is now **76.40**.

Surname ↑ First name	Email address	🐌 Task 1 ↓↑	🐌 Task 2 ↓↑	🐌 Task 3 ↓↑	x̄ Course total ↓↑
Ava B	AvaB@email.com	94.00 🔍	- 🔍	- 🔍	37.60
Emilie H	emilieH@email.com	99.00 🔍	- 🔍	- 🔍	39.60
Bayley W	BayleyW@email.com	91.00 🔍	100.00 🔍	- 🔍	76.40
Overall average		94.67	100.00	-	51.20

The calculation used in the simple weighted mean of grades is shown in the following table:

	Task 1	Task 2	Task 3	Total	Mean aggregation	Final grade shown in gradebook
Max grade possible	100	100	50	250		
Grade awarded	91.00	100.00	0	191	63.67	
normalized grade	0.91	1	0	1.91		
	(91/100)	(100/100)	(0/50)	(.91+1+0)		
Plus weighting	91	100	0	191	.764	76.40
	(.91*100)	(1*100)	(0*50)	(91+100+0)	(191/250)	(.764*100)

As previously, the grade awarded is normalized. However, in this aggregation method, this normalized grade is then multiplied by the maximum grade possible for the assessed activity. (In theory, the normalization process is not required in this aggregation type as the normalization and weighting calculations cancel each other back to the original grade awarded. However, in practice, Moodle always normalizes for this aggregation type). The mean aggregation calculation is, however, different in this method. Instead of dividing the normalized total by the number of grades in the course (in our previous example this was dividing the total by three), the simple weighted mean aggregation divides the normalized total by the total maximum grade possible (which is each of the maximum grades for each activity added together). In this case, it is dividing the normalized and weighted total by 250.

There is one final method of calculating a mean grade and this requires some additional options to be set by the teacher. Let's have a go at using the weighted mean of grades aggregation method.

Weighted mean of grades

In this method, each graded item in the course is manually given a weighting. In the mean of grades method, there is no weighting involved as it is a simple average calculation. In simple weighted mean of grades, the weighting is based on the maximum grade possible for each graded item. In weighted mean, the teacher sets the weighting within the gradebook.

An example use of this aggregation type could be when a specific assignment is worth more to the final course grade than others. For example, in our sample activities, **Task 1** and **Task 2** both have a maximum grade of 100. However, **Task 2** could have a lot of more detail and research required to complete the task and should, therefore, contribute more to the final grade than **Task 1**. With the simple weighted mean aggregation type, the two tasks will be treated equally. However, we can reflect the additional work within the final grade by making use of the weighting option within weighted mean of grades.

1. Go to **Categories and items** again.

2. Change the aggregation type to **Weighted mean of grades**.

   There are further changes that now need to be made here. Once weighted mean of grades has been chosen, a new column appears on the **Categories and items** page. This is the **Weight** column and allows us to apply a weight to each graded item. The default for each item is **1.0**. However, in this example **Task 2** has been changed to a weighting of 2.0 to reflect the additional work required when completing this activity.

3. Change the weighting of **Task 2** to **2.0** and click on **Save changes** at the bottom of the screen.

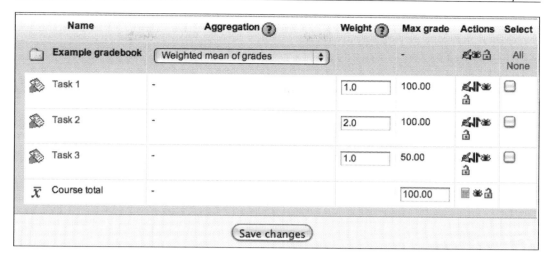

Let's see how this affects the final grade.

Switch back to view the gradebook. On the drop-down list at the top of the screen, find **View** and click on **Grader report** (or click on **View** on the tab at the top of the gradebook screen).

The course totals have changed again, so let's see how this is calculated. In this method of calculating a mean grade, each normalized grade is multiplied by the weight applied to that assessed item. The normalized grades are then added together and divided by the total weights applied to the course. The following table shows the calculations for this aggregation method for Bayley W's grades:

	Task 1	Task 2	Task 3	Total	Mean aggregation	Final grade shown in gradebook
Max grade possible	100	100	50			
Grade awarded	91.00	100.00	0	191	63.67	
Normalized grade	0.91	2	0	2.91	0.7275	72.75
	(91/100*1)	(100/100*2)	(0/50*1)	(0.91+2+0)	(1.91/4)	(.7275*100)

Note that Task 2 is multiplied by two as this is the weighting we applied for this assessed activity. The mean aggregation is calculated by dividing the total weighted normalized score by four, as this is the total number of weights applied to the course (that is a weighting of one for Task 1, a weighting of two for Task 2, and a weighting of one for Task 3).

We have seen three ways of calculating a mean grade within a course and also customizing the gradebook by choosing to include all assessed activities within the gradebook rather than just the marked activities. Another popular aggregation method is the **Sum of grades** calculation which acts differently to the normalized methods already discussed. Let's have a go with this aggregation method. We will also look at some other customizations available to change how the grade is displayed within the gradebook.

Example two – sum of grades

In this example, we will look at the sum of grades aggregation type. The course has five assignments to complete, each with a different final grade.

In the following screenshot, you can see how this example course has been set up:

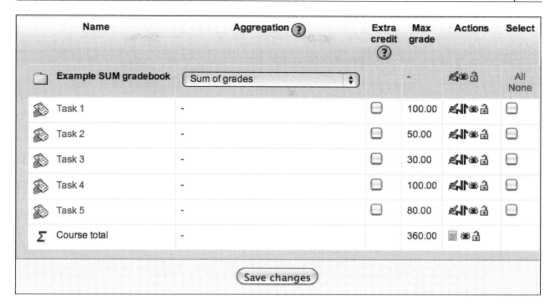

Name	Aggregation (?)	Extra credit (?)	Max grade	Actions	Select
📁 Example SUM gradebook	Sum of grades ⬍		-	🖊️🐾🔒	All None
🖍️ Task 1	-	☐	100.00	🖊️↕️👆🐾🔒	☐
🖍️ Task 2	-	☐	50.00	🖊️↕️👆🐾🔒	☐
🖍️ Task 3	-	☐	30.00	🖊️↕️👆🐾🔒	☐
🖍️ Task 4	-	☐	100.00	🖊️↕️👆🐾🔒	☐
🖍️ Task 5	-	☐	80.00	🖊️↕️👆🐾🔒	☐
Σ Course total	-		360.00	▤🐾🔒	

(Save changes)

Note the maximum grades for each assessed activity. The maximum grade for the course is the total of each assessed item within the course.

To change the aggregation type, you will use the same process as used previously.

1. Go into **Categories and items**.
2. Change the aggregation type to **Sum of grades** and click on **Save changes** at the bottom of the screen.
3. Now switch back to view the gradebook.

The calculation for this aggregation is simple. Each graded item is added together and presented as the course total grade. Normalization does not occur and it is not possible to exclude empty grades (unmarked items). This aggregation simply adds each item to the total as it is graded.

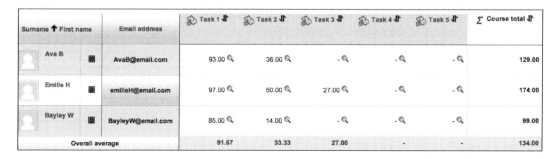

Surname ↑ First name		Email address	🖍️ Task 1 ↕️	🖍️ Task 2 ↕️	🖍️ Task 3 ↕️	🖍️ Task 4 ↕️	🖍️ Task 5 ↕️	Σ Course total ↕️
Ava B	🖼️	AvaB@email.com	93.00 🔍	36.00 🔍	- 🔍	- 🔍	- 🔍	129.00
Emilie H	🖼️	emilieH@email.com	97.00 🔍	50.00 🔍	27.00 🔍	- 🔍	- 🔍	174.00
Bayley W	🖼️	BayleyW@email.com	85.00 🔍	14.00 🔍	- 🔍	- 🔍	- 🔍	99.00
Overall average			91.67	33.33	27.00	-	-	134.00

However, it is possible to apply some **Extra credit** within this grade type.

Go back to the **Categories and items** page from within the grades area and notice the **Extra credit** column. For each graded item within the course, there is an option for it to be chosen for extra credit. So what does this do?

Any item that has extra credit applied to it is considered as an additional assessment and therefore, the maximum grade is not used in the course total.

For example, the course could have four required tasks. A student may not submit Task 2 on time, or get a sufficient grade, but they are not allowed to re-submit. Task 5 could be an additional, or alternative, task that can be used to increase the final course score. Another use of extra credit could be where the student has completed all work but has the option to improve their final grade by completing additional work.

In the example we are using, the course total is currently 360 which is calculated by adding all the maximum grades of each assessed item together. We are going to set Task 5 as **Extra credit**. This will mean that that the maximum grade of 80 is not included in the course total calculation. Let's apply this.

Go to the **Categories and items** screen and put a tick in the **Extra credit** column for **Task 5** and click on **Save changes** at the bottom of the screen.

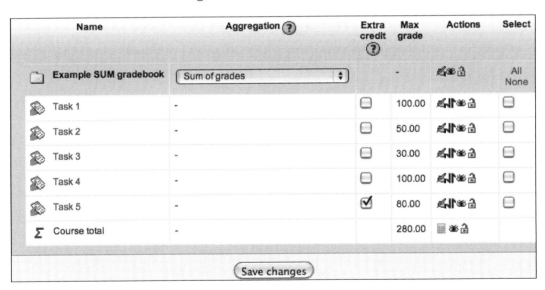

Note that the course total grade is now **280** instead of 360.

The maximum grade that a student can receive will always be 280. For example, if a student receives a grade of 100 in Task 1, 50 in Task 2, 30 in Task 3, 100 in Task 4, and also completes Task 5 and receives a grade of 80, their course total will still say 280 as it is not possible to get a grade higher than the course maximum. However, the extra credit will mean that students have an additional chance to receive the highest grade possible.

Viewing letter grades in the gradebook

Until now, we have been viewing the results in the gradebook as numbers.

In *Chapter 2, Customizing the Grades*, we created letter grades to show numbers as a corresponding word of our choice rather than the numbers we used to grade it (for example, Distinction instead of 100). We used the following percentages for the grade letters.

Letter grade	Highest percentage	Lowest percentage
Distinction	100%	100%
Merit	99.99%	75%
Pass	74.99%	50%
Not yet complete	49.99%	0%

If you are following these instructions within your own course, then make sure that you have the letter grades set up as shown previously. If you cannot remember how to do this, please refer back to *Chapter 2, Customizing the Grades*.

We can apply these to our gradebook so that instead of seeing a final number grade, we will see a word based on the percentage that the learner has received.

This takes some setting up!

1. Go to the **Grades** area (by clicking on **Settings and Grades**).
2. Go to **Categories and items** (either by clicking on the drop-down list and clicking on **Simple view** under the **Categories and items** heading or by clicking on **Categories and items** on the tabs bar).
3. Click on the edit icon at the top of the **Actions** column (next to the category aggregation drop-down list).
4. Make sure you are viewing the advanced options (if there is a button that says **Show advanced** on the right-hand side of the screen, click on it. If it says **Hide advanced** you are already viewing the advanced settings).

5. We are going to be using the **Category total** options towards the bottom of the screen.

6. Look for the **Grade display type** option. It probably says **Default (real)** in the current setting.

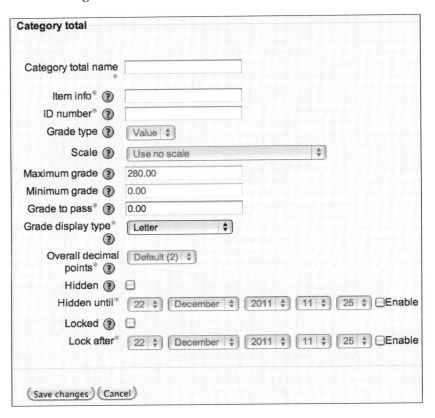

7. Click on the drop-down list and you will see a range of options. There are three main options:

   ◦ **Letter**: This shows the relevant letter grade in relation to the percentage set up in the letter grades options.

   ◦ **Percentage**: This will show the grade as a percentage. Moodle will calculate what the percentage grade is, based on the grade awarded and the maximum grade possible.

   ◦ **Real**: This will show the actual grade awarded in the grading process. This is what is currently showing as default.

You may notice that there are actually more than three options available in the drop-down list. You will see that there are options shown above plus another option in brackets. This allows you to choose two grades to be shown within the gradebook. For example, if **Letter (percentage)** is chosen the letter would be shown as the main grade in the gradebook and the corresponding percentage would be shown in brackets next to it.

From the drop-down list, choose **Letter** and click on **Save changes** at the bottom of the screen. Switch back to the gradebook **View** (**Grader report** in the drop-down list).

Take a look at the course total and note that the **Course total** column now has the words that have been set up as the letter grades. They are shown based on a calculated percentage grade, based on the work graded so far.

ne ↑ First name		Email address	🎲 Task 1 ↓↑	🎲 Task 2 ↓↑	🎲 Task 3 ↓↑	🎲 Task 4 ↓↑	🎲 Task 5 ↓↑	Σ Course total ↓↑
Ava B	▦	AvaB@email.com	93.00 🔍	36.00 🔍	- 🔍	- 🔍	- 🔍	Not yet complete
Emilie H	▦	emilieH@email.com	97.00 🔍	50.00 🔍	27.00 🔍	- 🔍	- 🔍	Pass
Bayley W	▦	BayleyW@email.com	85.00 🔍	14.00 🔍	- 🔍	- 🔍	- 🔍	Not yet complete
Overall average			91.67	33.33	27.00	-	-	Not yet complete

You can see that **Ava B** and **Bayley W** have not yet received sufficient grades to gain an actual grade yet (which means that they have received less than a 50 percent grade according to how our letter grades have been set up). As more work is completed and graded, the course total will increase and therefore the final grade will change.

Note that the tasks are still showing as real number grades. It is possible to change the settings for individual assignments to show alternative grade display types as well. Let's go in and change these!

1. Go back to **Categories and items**.
2. This time, click on the edit icon next to the first graded item on the list (in the example we have been using, this will be **Task 1**).
3. Find the **Grade display type** option and change it to **Letter**.
4. Click on **Save changes** at the bottom of the screen.
5. Repeat this process for all the assessed activities in the course (or as many as you want to show a letter grade instead of a number grade).

Take a look at the grader report again to see the letter grades instead of numbers shown in the gradebook.

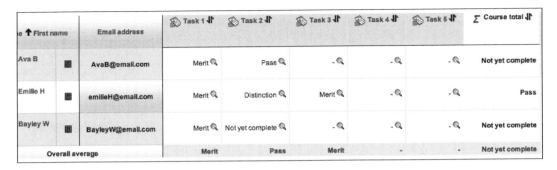

e ↑ First name		Email address	🎲 Task 1 ↓↑	🎲 Task 2 ↓↑	🎲 Task 3 ↓↑	🎲 Task 4 ↓↑	🎲 Task 5 ↓↑	Σ Course total ↓↑
Ava B	🔳	AvaB@email.com	Merit 🔍	Pass 🔍	- 🔍	- 🔍	- 🔍	Not yet complete
Emilie H	🔳	emilieH@email.com	Merit 🔍	Distinction 🔍	Merit 🔍	- 🔍	- 🔍	Pass
Bayley W	🔳	BayleyW@email.com	Merit 🔍	Not yet complete 🔍	- 🔍	- 🔍	- 🔍	Not yet complete
Overall average			Merit	Pass	Merit	-	-	Not yet complete

The process to change the way that the grades are displayed is the same for all types of aggregation and any graded activity. However, it always needs to be completed through the gradebook for each individual item so it could be quite time consuming for courses with lots of graded items.

If the course is going to use all the same grade display types, you can set the course default to an alternative (other than real, which is the current default).

Setting the course default for the grade display type

Within the **Grades** screen, we need to go to the **Settings** area (if using the drop-down list, find the **Settings** heading and click on **Course**. If using the tabs view, click on **Settings**).

Find the **Grade item settings** section and click on the drop-down list to change the default (real) option to the option you would like for the course. Save changes on this screen.

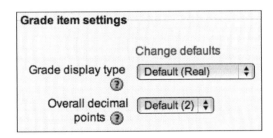

You will still be able to change each assignment type or total to an alternative grade display type, but all current and future graded activities will be presented as this chosen grade display type within the course.

Example three – using scales

So far we have been using the gradebook with number grades (and also choosing to view these as letter grades). However, courses may also use scales, which are often words for grading instead of numbers. In *Chapter 2*, *Customizing the Grades*, we set up a word scale for **Not yet complete**, **Pass**, **Merit**, and **Distinction**. When marking work, we pick one of these words as the grade.

Remember that scales have a simple scoring system based on the number of items in the scale rather than true numbers. Therefore, they are not always the best option for complex calculations. However, let's use some scales in the gradebook to see the calculations in action.

For this example, there are five tasks within the course and each one is graded on the PMD scale set up in *Chapter 2*, *Customizing the Grades* (with the following options for grading: Not yet complete, Pass, Merit, and Distinction).

You can see how these have been graded so far, in the following screenshot:

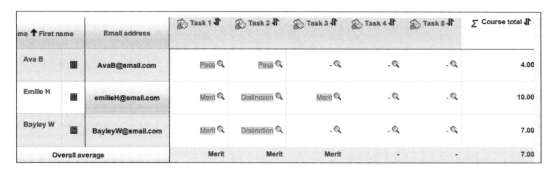

me ↑ First name		Email address	Task 1	Task 2	Task 3	Task 4	Task 5	Σ Course total
Ava B		AvaB@email.com	Pass	Pass	-	-	-	4.00
Emilie H		emilieH@email.com	Merit	Distinction	Merit	-	-	10.00
Bayley W		BayleyW@email.com	Merit	Distinction	-	-	-	7.00
Overall average			Merit	Merit	Merit	-	-	7.00

The course aggregation for this example, has been set to **Sum of grades**.

Remember, from *Chapter 2*, *Customizing the Grades*, the numbers that are used in calculations when using scales depends on the aggregation chosen. There were two ways in which a four-point scale (such as the one we are using) could be used. These two options are 0,1,2,3 or 1,2,3,4. Moodle decides which to use based on whether the aggregation type uses a normalized grading process or not. For normalized methods, the gradebook starts the scale scoring from zero.

However, the **Sum of grades** aggregation does not normalize the grades, so the scoring will start from one. In this four-point scale the grades will be one to four (Not yet complete = 1, Pass = 2, Merit = 3, and Distinction = 4).

Take a look at **Emilie H** in the previous screenshot. Her course total is **10**. This is calculated in the following way:

3 (Merit) + 4 (Distinction) +3 (Merit) = 10.

Let's change the aggregation type from **Sum of grades** to **Mean of grades** on the **Categories and items** screen. Also, make sure that the course total at the bottom of the screen says **100.00**. If it does not, then change the number and click on **Save changes** at the bottom of the screen. Go back to the **Grader** view to see how the course total has changed.

ne ↑ First name		Email address	Task 1	Task 2	Task 3	Task 4	Task 5	x̄ Course total
Ava B	▦	AvaB@email.com	Pass	Pass	-	-	-	33.33
Emilie H	▦	emilieH@email.com	Merit	Distinction	Merit	-	-	77.78
Bayley W	▦	BayleyW@email.com	Merit	Distinction	-	-	-	83.33
Overall average			Merit	Merit	Merit	.	.	64.81

Take a look at **Emilie H** again. This aggregation method uses a normalization process and the calculation is shown as follows. Remember, for normalized aggregation methods, scales start from 0 so the four-point scale will range from zero to three.

	Task 1	Task 2	Task 3	Total	Mean aggregation	Final grade shown in gradebook
Max grade possible	3 (for distinction)	3	3			
Grade awarded	2 (merit)	3 (distinction)	2 (merit)	7	2.333	
Normalized grade	0.6667 (2/3)	1 (3/3)	0.6667 (2/3)	2.3334 (.6667+1+.6667)	.7778 (2.3334/3)	77.78 (.7778*100)

This process will be the same for all normalized aggregation methods (with the aggregation calculation relevant to the method chosen).

Scales will always be based on the number of items in the scale and the gradebook will use the numbers either 0 or 1 (depending on the aggregation chosen) for the first item in the scale.

In these two examples, the course total has been shown as numbers. However, it is possible to set the course total to use the scale as well.

1. Go to the **Categories and items** area in the gradebook and click on the edit button next to the aggregation drop-down menu.

2. Make sure you can see the advanced options.

3. In the **Category total**, find the **Grade type** option and choose scale from the list.

4. This will activate the **Scale** drop-down list. From this list, choose the **PMD** scale which is the same scale used for the individual assessments.

5. Make sure the **Grade display** type says **Real** and **Save changes** at the bottom of the screen.

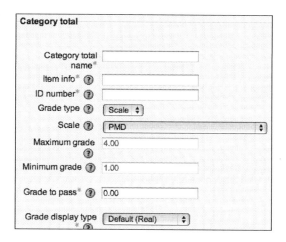

6. View the **Grader report** again.

You can see that the course total is now using the same scale as the graded items.

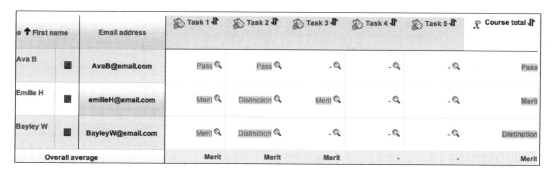

e ↑ First name		Email address	Task 1	Task 2	Task 3	Task 4	Task 5	x̄ Course total
Ava B	▦	AvaB@email.com	Pass	Pass	-	-	-	Pass
Emilie H	▦	emilieH@email.com	Merit	Distinction	Merit	-	-	Merit
Bayley W	▦	BayleyW@email.com	Merit	Distinction	-	-	-	Distinction
Overall average			Merit	Merit	Merit	-	-	Merit

The **Course total** scale uses the same scoring as the individual items and uses the aggregation method to decide which item of the scale to show.

Take a look at **Emilie H** again. Remember that the normalized total was **2.3334**. As two equates to **Merit** in this four-point scale, **Merit** is shown as the course grade. This example does not use the non-graded assessments in the total, so the grade will change as other work is completed. If the normalized grade is calculated as 0.5, the final grade will be rounded up. For example, Bayley W's normalized grade would be 2.5 (a grade of 2 for **Merit** and a grade of 3 for **Distinction** to make a total of 5. Divided by 2 for the number of grades in the mean calculation provides the 2.5 normalized total). This is rounded up to show a final course grade of **Distinction**.

Example four – using outcomes

We have seen a range of ways in which Moodle can use numbers, letters, and words to calculate the final course total. We will now look at how the outcomes we set in *Chapter 2, Customizing the Grades*, can be used in the course totals.

In this example, three assignment tasks have been set up with no grade, but each has a different outcomes applied to it. The outcomes are graded using the completion scale set up in *Chapter 2, Customizing the Grades*.

When marking this work, only the outcomes are graded (as either Not yet complete, Partially complete, or Complete). We will need to tell the gradebook to include outcomes in the grade aggregation.

For this example, students need to ensure that all assignment outcomes are complete so a lowest grade aggregation will be used. This is useful as all outcomes need to be marked as complete for the course to be complete. If there is one Not yet complete or Partially complete grade, this will be shown as the **Course total** and therefore teachers and students will know that some work still needs to be completed. Once all outcomes are graded as complete, the lowest grade will be complete and will be shown in the **Course total**. In order for these elements to be shown in the **Course total**, the **Course total grade type** needs to be the complete scale. This process requires a running total, based on all the required elements so the aggregation must include non-graded (empty) items in the gradebook.

There is one new element that needs to be applied here, in addition to the settings we have previously used. In the following instructions, onl y the new step (that is, choosing to include the outcomes in the grade aggregation) will be explained. The other steps will be stated, but you will need to use your previously learnt knowledge (or look back through previous pages) to apply them.

1. Go to the **Categories and items** screen.

2. Change the aggregation type to **Lowest grade**.

3. Click on the edit icon in the **Actions** column and ensure you can see the **Advanced settings**. In the **Grade category** section, remove the tick in the box next to **Aggregate only non-empty items** and click on the next box to add a tick next to **Include outcomes in aggregation**.

4. In the **Category total** section, ensure that the **Grade type** is set to **Scale** and choose the completion scale from the drop-down list.

5. Make sure the **Grade display type** is set to **Real**.

6. Scroll to the bottom of the screen and click on **Save changes**.

7. View the full grader report.

When using outcomes, the gradebook screen has a lot more information in it, as each outcome is listed as an additional column on the screen. Using lots of outcomes can make the gradebook a little difficult to use and will require some scrolling on your screen. However, you can see some of the items that have been graded and the course totals in the following screenshot:

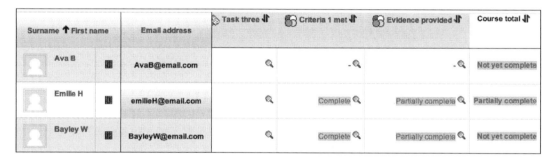

No grade will be shown in the main assignment column (**Task three** in the previous example) as it has been set up with no grade, but it does have two outcomes (shown with an interlocking circles icon) attached to it that are graded with a scale. While work is still being submitted and graded, the **Course total** will remain **Not yet complete**. Once a grade has been awarded to all outcomes, the lowest grade will be the one shown as the **Course total**.

Emilie H has submitted all her work and it has been graded, but there is still at least one element that is only partially completed which is reflected in her **Course total**. As mentioned previously, when using outcomes, the gradebook can have a lot of information on display. In the previous screenshot, Bayley W's **Course total** is shown as **Not yet complete** as there are outcomes that have not yet been graded which you cannot see in the screenshot, due to the number of items in the gradebook.

Summary

In this chapter, we have seen a range of ways in which the gradebook can be used to display student grades and calculate final course grades. We have seen how numerical grades and scales can be calculated to show a final course grade. We have also investigated how the different grading types and aggregation methods can be used.

With many options available in the gradebook, aggregation types can be quite confusing. However, having worked through the examples, you should now have a better understanding of the key settings related to the calculation of grades within the gradebook. This should give you an overall understanding of the aggregation types and settings available, but you can also use the chapter in future to apply the settings you need for your course.

In the next chapter, we will see how we can further customize the gradebook to organize grades into categories.

6
Organizing Using Categories

The gradebook can be difficult to use due to the amount of information shown within the table, especially in a course that uses a lot of graded activities. Often, the main course screen is arranged by topics to organize the content. We can apply a similar process to the gradebook through the use of categories to group grades by topic, assessment type, or other preferred arrangement.

We have seen how we can carry out course calculations based on how we want all the work added together. But what if you want unit one assignments to be calculated as a mean of grades and unit two to be the highest grade? What if you don't want some of the grades used in the calculations? These are other uses of categories. In this chapter, we will:

- Create categories and learn how to add graded activities into them
- See how categories can provide a range of aggregation types within one course
- See ways in which we can exclude grades from the final course total

Adding categories

Categories enable you to group graded activities within the gradebook so that they can be viewed together, and provide additional options for calculating final course grades. We will look at how they can be used throughout this chapter, but first we need to add some categories. We need to create the categories using the **Grades** area of the course.

1. Go to the **Grades** area via the Settings block on the main screen of the course, and to the **Categories and items** screen (if using the drop-down list you will need to choose **Simple view**).

2. At the bottom of the **Categories and items** screen, there is a button that says **Add category**. Click on this and a new screen will appear.

3. Give the category a name (such as Unit 1). Note that the options you get when setting up the category are the same as the options we used in *Chapter 5, Using Calculations*, to set up how the course should be aggregated. This includes the **Grade display type** as well as the **Aggregation method**. You can choose the same type of aggregation as the course or use one specific for this unit.

4. In the **Category total** section, you can set a **Maximum grade** for the category. Category totals will work in exactly the same way as the course total, in order to set a maximum grade available. For example, if Unit 1 has three assessments each worth 100 but the maximum for Unit 1 is 100, the maximum grade can be set and the aggregation will take this into account to present a final category total. Please see the following information box to know how this affects the course totals.

5. Make any further changes you would like for the category.

6. When you have added at least one category, you get an additional option at the bottom of the screen to choose a **Parent category**. This allows you to choose whether the category will be a main or a sub-category (a **sub-category** is a category nested within another category). We will look at a use of sub-categories later in the chapter.

7. Scroll to the bottom of the screen and click on **Save changes**.

When using categories, the course total is calculated by using the category totals instead of the individual assessment grades. The category will complete the aggregation as selected when it is created and present a category total. The course total will then use each category total in the aggregation that has been selected for the course total.

If the graded activities have already been added to the course, you can use the **Categories and items** screen to move graded activities into the relevant categories. Once categories have been set up, you can choose the relevant category when initially adding the graded activity to the course.

To move the graded activities into categories, put a tick next to each activity that you want to move (the **Select** column is on the right-hand side of the screen) and at the bottom of the screen click on **Move selected items to** and choose the category you would like them moved to. You can also use the standard move icon in the **Actions** column to move individual items as needed.

You can also move the order of the categories after they have been created by using the move icon.

1. Click on the move icon next to the category you want to move (in the **Actions** column). This will temporarily remove the category from the screen.

2. White boxes will appear on the screen in all the places where you can move the category to.

3. Click on the space where you would like the category to be.

In the following example, you can see that there are three categories within the course and there are two aggregation types used in the course.

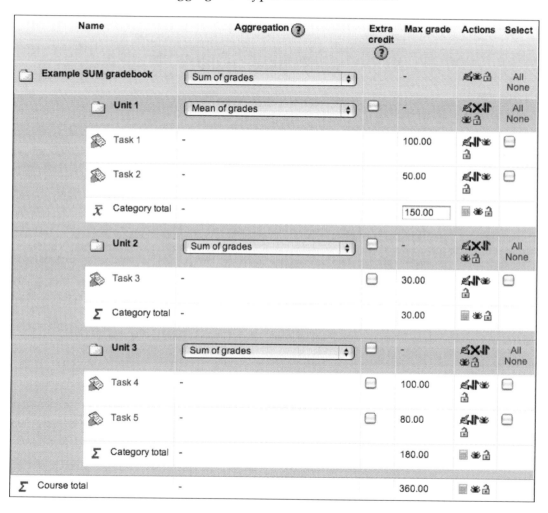

For this example, the total of **Unit 1** will be calculated using the **Mean of grades** aggregation type, which means the graded items will be divided by 2 (the total number of graded items in the category).

Unit 2 will present the **Sum of grades** (in this case, the total of one assignment) as the **Category total**.

Unit 3 will also show a **Sum of grades** of the two assignments as the **Category total**.

The **Course total** presented will be **Sum of grades** (as shown at the top of the screenshot), which will be a total of **Unit 1**, **Unit 2**, and **Unit 3**. The aggregation will use the category totals and will only use individual assessment grades if they are not in a category.

Excluding assessments from the final grade

There may be elements of the online course that are assessed, but they do not count towards a final grade. These could be formative assessments such as homework activities, quizzes to enable self-assessment, and so on. These graded items will automatically appear in the gradebook, but you may not want the grades to count in the final category or course total.

There are two main ways in which we can do this. One is to exclude a graded activity for all students, and the other is to exclude individual grades for each individual student.

Excluding assessments from aggregation for all students

There are two ways in which this can be achieved and both require the use of categories.

If you would like all the graded items that do not count towards the course total to be in one category, you can do the following:

1. Go to the **Grades** area and go to the **Categories and items** page.
2. Scroll to the bottom of the screen and click on **Add category**.
3. Give the category a name (such as 'formative assessments' or 'not used for final grade').
4. Make sure the aggregation is not **Sum of grades** (any other aggregation method is fine).

5. Make sure you can see the advanced options (it will say **Hide advanced** on the right-hand side of the screen).

6. In the **Category total** section, find the **Grade type** section and choose **None**.

7. Scroll to the bottom of the screen and click on **Save changes**.

Any graded activities that are listed in this category will not be included in the course total aggregation.

You could also create the same effect by creating a category with a **Category total** of zero.

If you would like to keep the formative work and the summative activities within the same category, rather than keeping all the formative work in a separate category, a sub-category could be used. This enables the graded items to appear together within the gradebook, but they are not counted in the **Course total** grade. To achieve this, you can do the following:

1. Go to the **Grades** area and go to the **Categories and items** page.

2. Firstly, go to the parent category (where you will be adding the sub-category) by clicking on the edit icon next to the category name.

3. Make sure that there is no tick next to the **Aggregate** including sub-categories. It is worth mentioning here that, if you are using sub-categories and you want the grades to be included in the **Course total**, you will need to go to the parent category and put a tick next to this option.

4. Click on **Save changes** at the bottom of the screen.

5. Scroll to the bottom of the screen and click on **Add category**.

6. Give the category a name (such as 'formative assessments' or 'not used for final grade').

7. Make sure the aggregation is not **Sum of grades** (any other aggregation method is fine).

8. Make sure you can see the advanced options (it will say **Hide advanced** on the right-hand side of the screen).

9. In the **Category total** section, find the **Grade type** section and choose **None**.

10. At the bottom of the screen, click on the drop-down list next to the parent category and choose the parent category that you edited previously.

11. Scroll to the bottom of the screen and click on **Save changes**.

Anything moved into this category will not be included in the course aggregation, but it will enable the work to be viewed within the gradebook with the relevant parent category.

Excluding assessments from aggregation for individual students

If we only want to exclude some grades for some students, you can do the following for each individual student for each graded activity:

1. Go into the **Grades** area (**Settings | Grades**).

2. At the top-right corner, click on **Turn editing on**.

3. Once editing is turned on, the edit icon will appear next to each individual graded item (it doesn't matter whether the work has been graded yet or not).

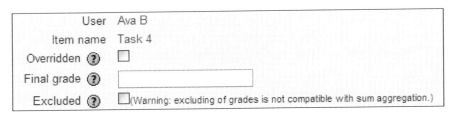

4. Click on the edit icon next to the activity that you would like to exclude from the aggregation.

5. A screen will appear with an option of **Excluded**. Click on the box next to this option to add a tick to the box.

6. Scroll to the bottom of the screen to click on **Save changes**.

These methods work with all aggregation types, except sum of grades. Sum of grades will always include all grades in the final aggregation. If you are using sum of grades, a warning appears next to the **Excluded** option reminding the user that **excluding of grades is not compatible with sum aggregation**.

Summary

In this chapter, we have seen some ways in which the gradebook can be organized to make it easier to use through the use of categories. Apart from grouping graded items together, categories can also be used to further increase the options for grade calculations by choosing the graded items in a category not to be included in the final grade. We have also seen how to exclude individual grades from the final course total.

In the next chapter, we will look at how we can use the information in the gradebook to report and review student achievement.

7
Reporting with the Gradebook

We have seen how we can use number, letter, and scale grades, and how to add assignments to courses. We can grade this work and we can set up the gradebook to calculate course totals.

We will now look at how we can view reports for all and for individual students, and some of the other ways in which the grade reports can be customized and exported. There are four main reports:

- Grader report
- Outcomes report
- Overview report
- User report

Grader report

We have already seen the grader report a few times throughout this book as it is the main screen we see when we go into the gradebook.

To get to the grader report we go into the Grades area.

- Click on **Grades** in the **Settings** block.
- If you are using the tabs layout, make sure that the **View | Grader report** are selected. If using the drop-down list to navigate the grades area, ensure that the **Grader report** under the **View** heading is selected.

You can see the tabs and drop-down menu in the following screenshot:

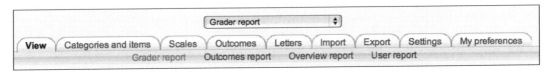

This report shows the grades for all the students for each graded activity. This enables the teacher to see the progress for all students in one place.

It shows one student per row, with the grade for each assignment in the columns across the table. However, with a lot of graded activities in the course, the grader report could be very wide. Categories can be used to organize this content, but the grader report also lets us collapse information to make it even easier to view.

There are three main ways to collapse the information. The following screenshot shows two rows of grades (for two different students) and there are three categories set up on this course (**Unit 1**, **Unit 2**, and **Unit 3**) as shown in the top row. Each category is displayed in a different way:

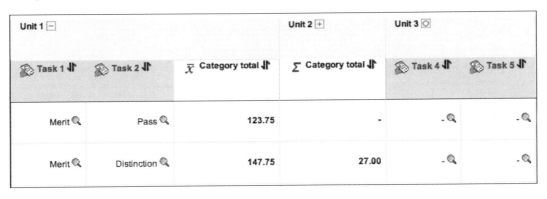

- **Unit 1** has a – symbol next to it. This is the default way of viewing the category and grade information. It shows each graded activity within the category (in this case, **Task 1** and **Task 2**) and the **Category total** column.

- **Unit 2** has a + symbol next to it. This only shows the **Category total** and not the graded activities that are in that category.

- **Unit 3** has a **o** symbol and this shows the graded activities within the category only and not the **Category total** column.

You can click on these symbols next to each category to toggle between each view. The changes are made for the individual user and will be remembered each time the user views the grader report. You can change the way the report is viewed at any time.

A useful option for courses with a lot of graded activities is to view the **Category total** only (so that the + symbol is showing). This will show all the category totals in the course so that the grader report is not too detailed. The user can then choose to view the full content of the category they are using at that point of time (such as the current unit being delivered). This is particularly useful for courses where different teachers teach different units, as they can collapse the categories so that they only view the category that they teach.

Another issue with a course, that has a lot of content, is related to having a lot of students on the course. This can make the table very long. This can be a particular issue if there are a number of course groups using the same online course. Again, different teachers may grade different groups of students. However, we can set up groups to enable teachers to only view the students they want.

Using groups to further improve gradebook use

Groups are a course-wide feature, but this section will give you a quick overview of how to set them up and use them within the gradebook.

There are three steps to using groups:

- Creating groups and adding students to them
- Setting the assignments to enable group views
- Changing the course settings to view groups in the gradebook

Creating groups

As groups can be used throughout the course, they need to be set up at course level rather than within the gradebook itself. Follow these instructions to create groups within your course:

1. Go to the main screen of the course and view the **Settings** block. Choose **Users** and click on **Groups**.
2. At the bottom of this screen, click on **Create group**.
3. Type in the name of the group (such as *Group A*) and click on **Save changes** at the bottom of the screen. Repeat this process for each group, as required.
4. After the groups have been created, they will appear in the groups list on the left-hand side of the screen. Click on the first group in the list so that it is highlighted and then click on **Add/remove users** in the bottom-right of the screen.

5. In the right-hand column on the screen, all current members of the course will appear. Choose the students who should be part of this group by clicking on their name and then clicking on **Add** in the centre of the two columns. Repeat this process for each student.

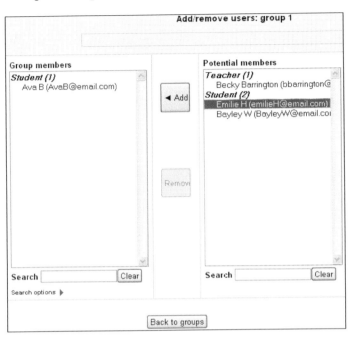

6. Once completed, click on **Back to groups** at the bottom of the screen. Repeat this process for other groups.

Enabling assignments to use groups

Each assignment that we want to be able to grade in groups has to be set up to enable the use of groups.

This is chosen in the common module settings of the assignment editing screen. This can be done when we initially set up the assignments We will amend an assignment that we have already created:.

1. When viewing the assignment on the screen click on **Edit settings** in the **Settings** block.

2. Find the **Group mode** option (in the **Common modules settings** section) and change the option from **No groups** to **Visible groups** and click on **Save and display the assignment**.

3. View the assignment and feedback grading area from within the assignment by clicking on **view submitted assignments** in the top right-hand side of the screen.

4. In the top-left of the assignment area, you will now see a **Visible groups** drop-down list:

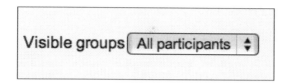

You can use this drop-down list to choose the group that you would like to view. This will filter the students and show only those students from the chosen group. You can still select **All participants** to see all the students on the grading screen.

Viewing groups in the gradebook

If we want to view these groups in the grader report, we need to change a course setting:

1. From the main course screen, go to the **Settings** block and click on **Edit settings**.

2. Scroll down the page and find the groups setting. Change the **Group mode** to **Visible groups**.

3. Scroll to the bottom of the screen and click on **Save changes**.

4. From the **Settings** block, click on **Grades** to go back to the **Grader report**.

5. You will notice that the **Visible groups** drop-down list is now available at the top of the grader report. Teachers can filter to view groups of students or view all students along with the relevant course grades.

The grader report will show the grade that each student has achieved for each activity and outcome but, as the grader report has a lot of information, it can be difficult for the teacher to see whether each outcome is being achieved within the course. However, the outcomes report provides a summary of the outcomes used in the course and shows the average outcome grades for the course, based on the outcome grades given to date.

Outcomes report

The outcomes report is used in courses where outcomes have been added to the course. If you have tabs at the top of your screen, click on **View** and then click on the **Outcomes report** under the tabs. If using the drop-down list, choose **Outcomes report** under the **View** heading (you can see both the drop-down list and tabs options at the top of the following screenshot).

The **Outcomes report** can help the teacher see which outcomes are being achieved, and at what level, and which ones may need additional support or development.

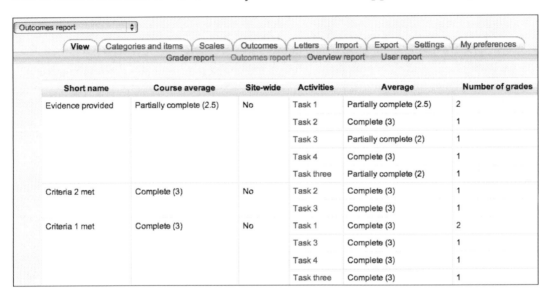

Short name	Course average	Site-wide	Activities	Average	Number of grades
Evidence provided	Partially complete (2.5)	No	Task 1	Partially complete (2.5)	2
			Task 2	Complete (3)	1
			Task 3	Partially complete (2)	1
			Task 4	Complete (3)	1
			Task three	Partially complete (2)	1
Criteria 2 met	Complete (3)	No	Task 2	Complete (3)	1
			Task 3	Complete (3)	1
Criteria 1 met	Complete (3)	No	Task 1	Complete (3)	2
			Task 3	Complete (3)	1
			Task 4	Complete (3)	1
			Task three	Complete (3)	1

This report shows the three outcomes that are used within this course listed in the first column titled **Short name**.

In the second column it shows the average grade for each outcome. This average is based on the grades awarded for the outcome divided by the number of times this outcome has been graded. The average is shown in the same scale as the outcome is graded in but the number in brackets is the equivalent number value. Remember that the numbers that scales use are based on the number of items in the scale. In this example, there are three options in the scale (not yet complete, partially complete and complete) which means the maximum number will be three. The average for 'evidence provided' is 2.5 and therefore will show the 'partially complete' scale value as this is item number two in the scale list. The other two outcomes are both shown as complete, which is the third item in the scale list, as the average grade is 3.

The **Site-wide** column will state yes or no depending on whether the outcome is used in this course only (in which case it will say No) or if the outcomes are used throughout the Moodle site (in which case it will say Yes).

The final three columns provide the additional details for how the outcomes are used. The **Activities** column shows each activity which has this outcome assigned. The **Average** column will show the average grade for that task and the final **Number of grades** column shows how many grades this average is based on.

Overview report

The next report available is the overview report. (If you have tabs at the top of your screen, click on **View | Overview report**. If using the drop-down list, choose **Overview report** under the **View** heading.) This can be accessed from any course, but it enables a teacher to view the current course totals for each student on all the courses in which they are currently enrolled on Moodle.

After clicking on **Overview report** a list of courses will appear, but the first step is to choose a user, or student, for which we want to see the current course results. This drop-down list appears on the right-hand side next to **Select a user**:

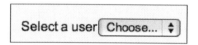

Once a user has been chosen, the course list will change and show all the courses that the chosen student is enrolled on and the grade column will show the current grade awarded for each course.

Course name	Grade
Outcomes	Not yet complete
Scales	Distinction
Number grades	Not yet complete
NumberMean	72.75
test	258.00
LetterGrades	Pass

The grade shown is the same grade that appears in the **Course total** column of the grader report for each individual course. This grade is likely to change throughout the duration of the course.

The overview report enables teachers to view a student's progress across a number of Moodle courses without the need to visit each course individually. However, the teacher can choose to review the details of the individual student's progress by clicking on the course name in the overview list. This will show the user report for the learner for the chosen course.

User report

You can access the user report in the same way as the grader and overview reports. If using the drop-down list, find the **View** heading and click on **User report**. If using the tabs menu, click on **View | User report**.

Similar to the overview report, the user report requires the teacher to choose a user from the drop-down list on the right-hand side (unless the user report is accessed through the overview report or by clicking on the grades icon next to the student name in the grader report).

The user report will show each graded activity in the course along with the current grade awarded for each activity and the feedback given. This has the same information as the grader report, but for an individual student. It also presents the information in a portrait rather than landscape format (the following screenshot only has a few activities within the gradebook, but for courses with a lot of graded activities the page will be longer).

Grade item	Grade	Range	Percentage	Feedback
Scales				
Task 1	Merit	Not yet complete–Distinction	66.67 %	Good work
Task 2	Distinction	Not yet complete–Distinction	100.00 %	Excellent work
Task 3	-	Not yet complete–Distinction	-	
Task 4	-	Not yet complete–Distinction	-	
Task 5	-	Not yet complete–Distinction	-	
Assignment one	-	Not yet complete–Distinction	-	
Assignment two	-	0–30	-	
Attendance grade	-	0–100	-	
Course total	*Distinction*	*Not yet complete–Distinction*	*100.00 %*	

The user report shows each graded activity from the course in the **Grade item** column, with the current **Grade** awarded next to it.

The **Range** column shows the lowest and the highest grade that can be achieved from the assignment, and the **Percentage** column shows the grade as the equivalent percentage. Finally, the **Feedback** column shows the full written feedback given for the activity.

Grade Item	Grade	Range	Percentage	Feedback
Example gradebook				
Task 1	91.00	0–100	91.00 %	Very good Bayley
Task 2	100.00	0–100	100.00 %	Excellent work Bayley. Well done.
Task 3	-	0–50	-	
$\bar{x}$ Course total	72.75	0–100	72.75 %	

The final row of the column shows the **Course total** grade so far, this is the same information as shown in the **Course total** column in the grader report and in the overview report. In the previous screenshot, this is **72.75** (this course is calculated as the weighted mean).

Which reports do students see?

A student can access the gradebook in the same way as a teacher. They will click on **Grades** in the **Settings** block.

When a student views their grades, it is their own user report that they will see. Students can also view the overview report. Both reports look the same for the students as they do for the teacher. However, they can only see their own reports, whereas a teacher can view the reports for all students on the course.

By default the gradebook is available for students to view. If you would like to turn off access to the grades for students, you can do this in the course settings. (From the main course screen, go to the **Settings** block and click on **Edit settings**. In the **General** section, find **Show gradebook to students,** and change this from **Yes** to **No**).

Customizing the reports view

We have seen how the grader, outcomes, overview, and user reports can be used and the information that can be shown on each of them. The information shown in the screenshots used are based on the default settings of each report. However, each of the reports can also be customized to change the information shown.

For example, if the percentage column is not needed in the user report, then this can be hidden. Within the **Grades** area of the course, there is a **Settings** section that can be used to change how each report is viewed on the course.

This is accessed through the **Settings** tab (if using the tabs layout) or click on the drop-down list, find the **Settings** heading, and click on **Course** (if using the drop-down list option).

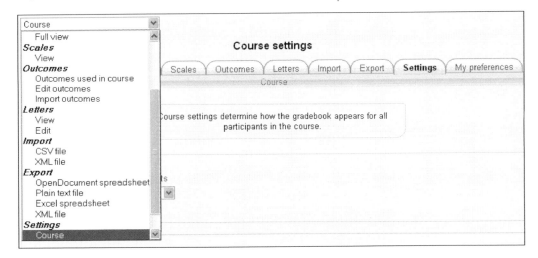

A range of options available for each type of report is shown in the following screenshot:

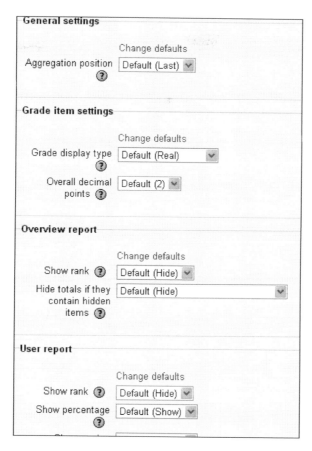

Change the settings to meet your needs and click on **Save changes** at the bottom of the screen. These settings will be applied to the course rather than the individual user.

Exporting the gradebook data

Apart from viewing the data within Moodle, it is possible to export the gradebook data and download to view and use it offline. There are four options for downloading:

- Open document spreadsheet
- Plain text file
- Excel spreadsheet
- XML file

You access these options from the **Grades** area, in Moodle, in the same way as accessing the reports. How you access the export options will depend on whether you are using the drop-down menu or tab navigation within the **Grades** area. Both options are shown in the following screenshot:

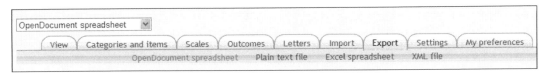

If using the drop-down menu, find the **Export** heading and click on **OpenDocument spreadsheet** (or you can also choose other export options from here).

If using the tabs layout, click on the **Export** tab. Within the **Export** tab, a second row of options appear which provides the export options. Once you are in the export screen, a range of options are available for choosing the information to export and download.

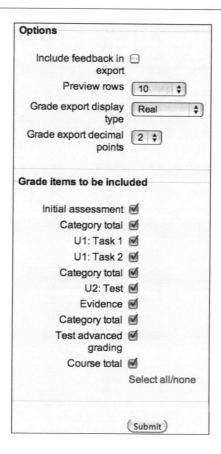

- **Include feedback in export**: This will include the written feedback alongside the exported data. To include this, we need to click on the box to add a tick.

- **Preview rows**: This allows us to choose the number of rows of student data that will be shown once the options are submitted. This allows the teacher to check the data to ensure it shows the information required, before finally exporting the information.

- **Grade export display type**: The teacher can choose whether the real, percentage, or letter grade is the grade shown in the exported data and how many decimal points are shown with the **Grade export decimal points** option.

- **Grade items to be included**: The second part of the options will show all the graded activities, category totals, and the course total that are included in the online course. The teacher can choose which elements they would like in the exported data. For example, a teacher may only want to export the data for their own unit. A tick in the box will indicate that the data is to be exported. All items will be ticked by default. Clicking on the tick will remove the tick and therefore will not include the data in the export.

- Click on **Submit** to start the export process.

After clicking on **Submit**, a preview screen will appear with a **Download** button on it:

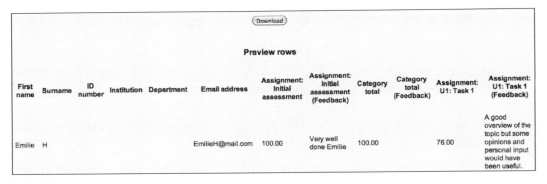

The **Download** button will download the chosen gradebook data in the selected format.

Summary

In this chapter we have seen the range of ways in which the gradebook can be used and customized to show the data required for both teachers and students.

Teachers can see all student grades and individual user data as well as set up groups to aid the marking and review process. Students and teachers can also see an overview of all the courses that a user is enrolled on to see the current final grade for each course.

These reports provide the main options for viewing grades. However, there are a few further customizations that can aid progress tracking. The final chapter will outline some of these options to further enable the tracking of learner progress.

8
Additional Features for Progress Tracking

The gradebook is a very useful tool to manage the progress of students. It enables teachers to review and manage the grades awarded for each graded activity in the course. However, there are also some other functions within Moodle that enable the gradebook to be further enhanced or to track progress outside of the gradebook. In this chapter, we will:

- Set pass grades to visually show achievement and progression for individual pieces of work
- Turn on activity tracking to show progress through activities on the course
- Use course completion to track progress through required elements of the course
- Use course and activity completion reports

Setting pass grades

As we know, we can view the grades awarded in the gradebook. However, we can also set pass levels for each graded activity to provide a visual view within the gradebook. When pass grades are set, the gradebook will not only show the grade, but a background color will also be applied. If the grade awarded is below the pass grade, the background color will be red. If the grade awarded is at or above the pass grade, the background color will be green.

This option is set from within the gradebook and needs to be set for each individual activity. We will now do this for the assignments we set up earlier.

1. Go to the gradebook by clicking on **Settings | Grades**.

2. Go to the **Simple view** of the **Categories and items** section of the gradebook.

 You can also complete these tasks by turning editing on within the grader report and clicking on the edit icon below the graded item.

3. Click on the edit icon (probably a hand holding a pen in the **Actions** column) next to the graded item for which you would like to set the pass grade.

4. We need to use the advanced options: click on **Show advanced** on the right-hand side (if the button says **Hide advanced** then you are already viewing the advanced options).

5. You will see the **Maximum grade** option that was set when the activity was first created, along with the **Minimum grade** option. Beneath these two options, there is the **Grade to pass** setting. By default, the grade to pass is **0** but in the following example the pass grade has been set as **95.00**:

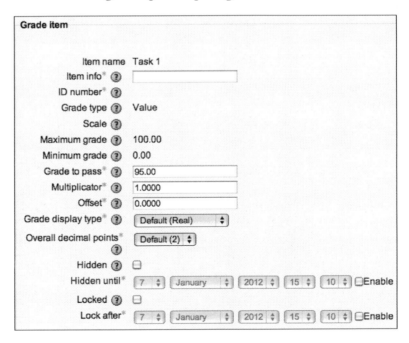

6. Click on **Save changes** at the bottom of the screen.

Once you have saved the grade to pass, return to **Grader report**. You will now notice that there is a background color for any grades that have been awarded for this assignment.

In the following screenshot, two of the grades are below the pass grade (**Ava B** and **Bayley W**). On the Moodle screen, these are shown with a red background. However, **Emilie H** has received a grade above the pass grade and her grade will be shown with a green background on the Moodle screen.

Surname ↑ First name		Email address	🗞 Task 1 ⬍
Ava B	▦	AvaB@email.com	94.00 🔍
Emilie H	▦	emilieH@email.com	99.00 🔍
Bayley W	▦	BayleyW@email.com	91.00 🔍

Adding pass grades, where relevant, can help the teacher to quickly see how learners are progressing when viewing the grades. However, setting pass grades can also be useful in other areas of Moodle as well.

Activity tracking

Activity tracking in Moodle allows students and teachers to track their use of resources and activities, and this information can be shown to students on the Moodle screen and in a report for teachers. It can also be used as one of the criteria towards determining course completion status.

Activity and completion tracking is a major new feature within Moodle 2.x and there are a range of options available with it. Activity tracking can be set for any resource within the course. It allows students and teachers to easily see which work has been viewed or completed. Each item within the course needs to be set to enable activity tracking so you can choose for some items to be tracked while others are not. For the purpose of this chapter we are only going to set assignments to be tracked, but the instructions are the same for all Moodle resources and activities.

In order for activity tracking to be used, it needs to be turned on in site administration and course administration.

Site administrators can find the option in **Site administration | Advanced features** and they need to tick the box to enable completion tracking.

Once completion tracking is turned on for the Moodle site, teachers can turn on the option within the course by going to the **Settings** block and clicking on **Edit settings** under the **Course administration** heading. Once on this screen, we need to scroll down to find the **Student progress** section. Next to **Completion tracking** change the option from **Disabled** to **Enabled**. You will also notice a **Completion tracking begins on enrolment** option. At the time of writing, this option does not affect the completion tracking progress. Activity tracking begins when any user starts to use the online course whether they are enrolled or not. It is expected that this option will be removed in future versions.

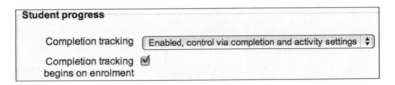

Click on **Save changes** at the bottom of the screen. We can now add activity tracking to any resource or activity within the course. We have already set an assignment to have a pass grade, so now we will also add activity tracking to it to see how this enables us to check progress.

1. View the assignment on the screen and click on **Edit settings** in the **Settings** block.

2. Scroll down to find the **Activity completion** section at the bottom of the screen.

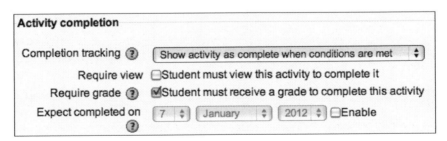

3. The **Completion tracking** drop-down list will have three options:

    ◦   **Do not indicate activity completion**: The resource will appear on the Moodle course as it does in Moodle 1.x.

- ○ **Students can manually mark as complete**: Students will tick the activity to show that they have viewed or completed it. This is often a good choice for Moodle resources where you want to track whether the student has read the content. For example, the student ticks the activity to say they have read it as Moodle can only tell if a student has clicked on the link.

- ○ **Show activity as complete when conditions are met**: Moodle will indicate whether the resource or activity has been completed or not. Depending on the type of activity, the options for completion will vary. This is the often the best option to choose for Moodle activities where specific tasks need to be completed.

4. Choose **Show activity as complete when conditions are met**.

5. The options below the drop-down list are the different ways in which Moodle can decide whether the activity is completed or not. The options will vary depending on the type of activity. All resources and activities will have the **Student must view this activity to complete it** option. However, as an assignment is a graded activity, we also get the option of **Student must receive a grade to complete this activity**. Put a tick in the box to choose this option.

6. Scroll to the bottom of the screen and click on **Save and return to course**.

Take a look at the course screen and you will now notice a tick icon on the right-hand side of the assignment:

The icon indicates that the resource has activity completion settings associated with it. This icon is viewed by individual students to show their progress through the course. By default, as soon as the assignment is graded, the activity will be marked as complete. However, as we have set a grade to pass, the activity will only be marked as complete when the assignment is graded at or above the pass grade.

Reporting

Let's take a look at how students and teachers view the activity completion information.

Student view

Students view their progress through the main course screen. Next to each item that has activity completion set up, the student will see a tick once the item has been completed. In the case of assignments with **Grade to pass** set, the student will see a tick when the assignment has been graded at the pass grade or higher. If the student does not gain the minimum grade to pass, a cross will appear next to the resource.

The following screenshot shows **Task 1** on the main course screen when Emilie H is logged in:

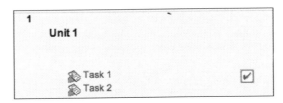

A tick is shown next to **Task 1,** which shows that Emilie has completed this task through achieving at least the minimum grade to pass.

However, the following screenshot shows Bayley W's course screen with the same task with a cross next to it to indicate that the assignment has been graded but it has not yet met the required pass grade. This shows that the activity is not yet complete.

The individual course screen, and completion status of each activity, will vary for each student. However, the teacher will want to see all the completion information on one screen.

Teacher view

Teachers view students' progress through the **Activity completion** report, which will show the activity completion status for each student on the course for each activity that has the activity completion turned on. To get to this report, we need to use the **Navigation** block.

Within the **Navigation** block, we have a **My courses** list which will show all the courses which we are enrolled on, either as a teacher or a student.

 For administrators, the name of this list changes to **Courses** when they are within a Moodle course.

When we are in a course, the current course should be expanded to show further options within the navigation menu. In the following screenshot, we can see that we are currently using the course called **Gradebook** (this is the short name for the course and is the same name as shown in the navigation breadcrumb pathway at the top on the course screen).

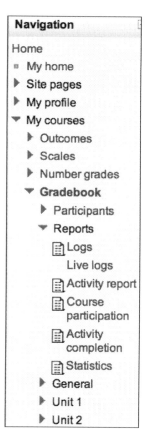

We need to click on **Reports** to view the different reporting options for the course. The report we need to use is **Activity completion**. After clicking on this option, we will see a screen similar to the one shown as follows:

First name / Surname	Email address	Task 1	Revision website	Task 2	Introduction to the unit	Useful glossary of terms	Topic i
Ava B	AvaB@email.com	✗	☐	▨	☐	☐	
Emilie H	emilieH@email.com	✓	☐	▨	☐	☐	
Bayley W	BayleyW@email.com	✗	☐	✓	☐	☐	

Visible groups: All participants

First name: **All** A B C D E F G H I J K L M N O P Q R S T U V W X Y Z
Surname: **All** A B C D E F G H I J K L M N O P Q R S T U V W X Y Z

First name: **All** A B C D E F G H I J K L M N O P Q R S T U V W X Y Z
Surname: **All** A B C D E F G H I J K L M N O P Q R S T U V W X Y Z

- Download in spreadsheet format (UTF-8 .csv)
- Download in Excel-compatible format (.csv)

There are many resources within the course, but this report will only show resources and activities where the activity completion has been set. We can see each student on the course listed on the left-hand side, and the activities that have activity completion settings added to them will appear across the top of the screen. This table will show the current completion status for each student for each activity.

In the previous screenshot, we can see that one student has currently passed **Task 1** and two students have not yet passed. If the assignment had not yet been submitted for any student, or it had not been graded, there would be no color icon in the activity column (as shown for **Ava B** and **Emilie H** for **Task 2**. Cross icons only appear when **Grades to pass** have been set.

This activity report enables the teacher to very quickly see progress on required items in the course. When used with the **Grade to pass** option, the teacher can very easily view how individual students are progressing in a simple format. It does not, however, provide the specific grade for each assignment so it does not completely replace the gradebook. We can click on the activity name in the top row of the activity completion report and this will take us to the activity (and access to the grades) if required. However, in courses, where students only need to reach a certain level to complete the course, the activity completion report could be used instead of the gradebook for progress tracking.

You will notice that it is possible to choose letters for **First name** and **Surname** to filter the group to see specific students. If groups are set up for use in the course, the groups' list will also appear in this activity completion report, to filter groups of students. You can also download this data into a spreadsheet for further use and manipulation.

If courses have lots of resources with activity completion added, this report can be quite long and wide. However, it is possible to further select activities for reporting, through the use of course completion.

Course completion

Course completion enables the teacher to set the required elements that must be completed in order to complete the course. This can be used in the same way as the activity completion, but it can also be used to complement it.

For example, the online course may contain a wide range of resources and activities that could be a mixture of required elements, alongside further supplementary resources. However, some of these activities, such as the assessed elements, may need to be tracked separately by the teacher, and looking through the whole activity report could be quite time consuming. This is where course completion can be used.

Within the course, where course completion is to be added, click on the **Settings** block and click on **Completion tracking**.

 This needs to be enabled within the course first as explained in the *Activity tracking* section of this chapter.

The completion settings that we will be changing are **Manual completion by** and **Activities completed**, and the changes to make are as follows. However, each section is explained for information:

- **Overall criteria type aggregation**: This is where we can choose whether all the activities that are chosen as required elements need to be completed, or if any of them can be completed (in which case, as long as one of them is completed, the student will complete the course).

- **Course prerequisites**: If other courses on the site have course completion set up, we can choose other courses that need to be completed before this course can be set as complete. Students can work on the online courses concurrently, but the course where this setting is enabled will not be marked as complete until the chosen prerequisite courses are also marked as complete.

- **Manual self completion**: Put a tick in the box if the student is able to indicate when they believe that they have completed the course.

If using this option the self-completion block must also be added to the course to give students the link to choose to **Complete course**.

- **Manual completion by**: This can be used as a final checking procedure. If a role is chosen here, any user with that role will need to check all the activities and manually confirm that the work is completed. This is very useful where additional paperwork or checking is required. For our example, choose **Teacher**.

- **Activities completed**: All resources and activities that have activity completion added to them will appear in a list here with a tick box next to them. It is here that we will choose the required elements that need to be achieved in order to complete the course. For our example, this is all the assignments within the course. Put a tick next to each assignment in your course.

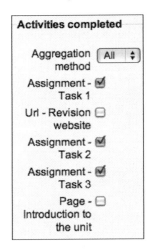

- **Date**: If enabled, students will not be able to complete the course until at least the date set.

- **Duration after enrolment**: If enabled, students will not be able to complete the course until at least the mentioned number of days from which they became a member of the online course.

- **Grade**: If enabled, a course pass grade can be set. Once the gradebook course total meets this grade for a student, they will be marked as complete on the course completion report.

- **Unenrolment**: If enabled, when the student is unenrolled from the course it will be assumed that they have completed the course.

- Click on **Save changes**.

Reporting

It is possible to access the course completion report through the **Reports** option within the **Navigation** menu in the same way as the activity completion report. However, there is also a block available to further enhance the use of course completion.

Follow these steps to add the block:

1. Click on **Turn editing on**.
2. On the right-hand side of the screen, find the **Add a block** option and click on **Add**.
3. Choose **Course completion status**.

Teacher view

For the teacher, the block will look like the following:

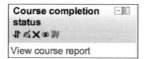

Click on **View course report**.

You will see a similar report to the activity completion report, but it will only show the options, resources, and activities that were chosen in the **Completion tracking** setup process.

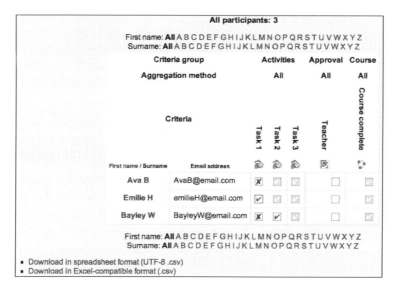

The report shows ticks for **Activities** that have been completed successfully, or a cross where a student has not yet met the specific requirements for the activity and has not been awarded the required pass grade. There will be no icon shown for the activities that are not yet complete.

Under **Approval**, there is a **Teacher** column. This is used by the teacher to manually tick when they are satisfied that all the required elements have been completed. If no role is set up for manual completion, this column will not be in the course report.

If self completion has been turned on, this will also be shown here.

Finally, the **Course** heading has a **Course complete** column. When there is a tick in each column for the learner, a tick will automatically appear in this column.

 If any course prerequisites or course pass grades have been set in the **Completion tracking** screen, these elements will be shown in the report.

As with the activity completion report, you can view specific students, download the report, and use groups on this screen.

Student view

A student will see a different version of this report and, of course, it will only show their own data. Let's take a look at what Bayley W would see.

On the main screen of the course, Bayley sees a summary of his progress to date in the **Course completion status** block:

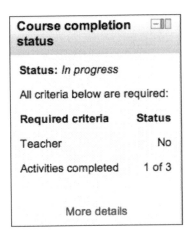

Bayley can see that the course is currently in progress and that one of the three required activities is complete. Bayley can get further information by clicking on **More details**.

| | | Status: *In progress* | | | |
| | | Required: All criteria below are required | | | |

Criteria group	Criteria	Requirement	Status	Complete	Completion date
Activities completed	Task 1	Achieving grade		No	-
(*all* required)	Task 2	Achieving grade		Yes	9 January 2012
	Task 3	Achieving grade		No	-
Manual completion by	Teacher	Marked complete by Teacher		No	-

This provides further information about the requirement for completing the activities and the current status of each item required. If complete, the completion date is shown.

When using this option the self completion block must also be added to the course. This block contains one link: **Complete course**. This is clicked on when the student is ready to complete the course (that is, when they feel that everything is finalized and complete). The student will be asked to confirm by clicking on **Yes** or **No**. Please note that students can click on this even if the required course activities are not yet complete.

If self completion is enabled for the course, students will also see a self-completion option within this report.

The activity and course completion reports are updated when the cron job is completed on the server. This captures the most up to date information in relation to Moodle activities to ensure the reports are up to date. If the reports need to be constantly up to date, the cron job may need to be set up to run regularly. Speak to your Moodle administrator to find out more about the cron job.

Summary

These activity and course completion options can be used to complement the gradebook or, in courses where the gradebook itself may be too complex to review, can be used to show a simpler view of elements that the student has achieved to date. The teacher can choose the specific resources and activities that they want to be able to report on regularly, but still use the gradebook for additional detail. In addition, we have seen how course completion settings can be used to monitor the completion of essential elements within a course.

This book has shown some of the key ways in which the gradebook can be used to manage learning and monitor progress through a course, for both teachers and students. The gradebook is a complex and sophisticated tool and has some further advanced functions for calculating final grades. However, the preset options still provide a wide range of functions and we have explored a range of ways in which the gradebook can be customized to meet specific needs.

I really hope that you have found this book useful and, more importantly, identified some potential uses for your online courses that you can apply to aid your day-to-day management of online learning.

Keep experimenting, playing, and trying new ideas; but most of all, happy Moodling!

Index

Thank you for buying
Moodle Gradebook

About Packt Publishing

Packt, pronounced 'packed', published its first book "*Mastering phpMyAdmin for Effective MySQL Management*" in April 2004 and subsequently continued to specialize in publishing highly focused books on specific technologies and solutions.

Our books and publications share the experiences of your fellow IT professionals in adapting and customizing today's systems, applications, and frameworks. Our solution based books give you the knowledge and power to customize the software and technologies you're using to get the job done. Packt books are more specific and less general than the IT books you have seen in the past. Our unique business model allows us to bring you more focused information, giving you more of what you need to know, and less of what you don't.

Packt is a modern, yet unique publishing company, which focuses on producing quality, cutting-edge books for communities of developers, administrators, and newbies alike. For more information, please visit our website: www.packtpub.com.

About Packt Open Source

In 2010, Packt launched two new brands, Packt Open Source and Packt Enterprise, in order to continue its focus on specialization. This book is part of the Packt Open Source brand, home to books published on software built around Open Source licences, and offering information to anybody from advanced developers to budding web designers. The Open Source brand also runs Packt's Open Source Royalty Scheme, by which Packt gives a royalty to each Open Source project about whose software a book is sold.

Writing for Packt

We welcome all inquiries from people who are interested in authoring. Book proposals should be sent to author@packtpub.com. If your book idea is still at an early stage and you would like to discuss it first before writing a formal book proposal, contact us; one of our commissioning editors will get in touch with you.

We're not just looking for published authors; if you have strong technical skills but no writing experience, our experienced editors can help you develop a writing career, or simply get some additional reward for your expertise.

Moodle 2.0 Course Conversion Beginner's Guide

ISBN: 978-1-84951-482-8   Paperback: 368 pages

A complete guide to successful learning using Moodle 2

1. Move your existing course notes, worksheets, and resources into Moodle quickly

2. No need to start from scratch! This book shows you the quickest way to start using Moodle and e-learning, by bringing your existing lesson materials into Moodle

3. Demonstrates quick ways to improve your course, taking advantage of multimedia and collaboration

Moodle 1.9 for Teaching 7-14 Year Olds: Beginner's Guide

ISBN: 978-1-847197-14-6   Paperback: 236 pages

Effective e-learning for younger students using Moodle as your Classroom Assistant

1. Focus on the unique needs of young learners to create a fun, interesting, interactive, and informative learning environment your students will want to go on day after day

2. Engage and motivate your students with games, quizzes, movies, and podcasts the whole class can participate in

3. Go paperless! Put your lessons online and grade them anywhere, anytime

Please check **www.PacktPub.com** for information on our titles

Made in the USA
Lexington, KY
01 June 2013